HOME ON EARTH

Recipes for Healthy Houses

Photos by Ty Cole

BLDUS

ORO EDITIONS

HOME ON EARTH

Recipes for

BLDUS

Healthy Houses

TABLE OF CONTENTS

FRONT OF HOUSE

Too Low They Build, Who Build Beneath the Stars.

- Library of Congress Inscription
by Edward Young

Architecture: marking where humans seek refuge between Earth and sky; mitigating the heat of the golden Sun; mediating the tides and clouds; infused with auras reflective of formative human spirits; revealing relationships between material elements, human habitation, and the metaphysical Cosmos. Like doctors and their patients, lawyers and their clients, and chefs and their guests, architects engage with a general public that knows certain aspects of their profession personally due to the fundamental nature of the discipline. Everyone has a relationship to space, and even to spacemaking; it's part of our common condition as humans. People are born into spaces, spend their lives in built spaces, and die in built spaces. The prototypical spaces of a civilization resonate through time, becoming some of humanity's most cherished cultural constructions.

This book is an epicurean treatise on the culinary art of architecture: a book of recipes for healthy houses, designed for a specific region—the hills, valleys, and back alleys of Washington, DC, and the broader Mid-Atlantic. These twelve houses stand between memorials and monuments: the spaces between the stars. Like any cuisine, this set of material assemblies is born of its regional identity through its local ingredients and response to climate, yet each of these dishes can be studied for their applications and implications in other regions. All were prepared by BLDUS, a DC-based architecture practice. Make yourself at home on Earth.

HOME COOKING

Located in the capital city of the United States on residual parcels amidst historic urban settings, the six houses shown here received particular care throughout their design and construction to achieve passive durability. The healthy systems, techniques, and technologies they employ require minimal maintenance and energy inputs.

Each of these houses advocate in their own way for healthy building materials that work well in the ecology of the Mid-Atlantic region and have low impacts on their points of growth, manufacture, installation, inhabitation, and eventual reintegration with the Earth. Regional materials like tulip poplar bark and sassafras wood complement globally produced high-performing products like bamboo-wood hybrid frames with hollow wall cavities, sheep's wool insulation, and cork cladding. The application of each material is carefully thought through in order to be easy to make, and maintain, and enjoy.

Like local chefs, we trust our taste, and like the national farm-to-table movement in cooking, natural architecture can lead to healthier lives, but unlike chefs' dishes, architecture must provide enduring shelter, demanding unique ways of fostering health at home through building. With shorthand details explaining how to assemble lists of ingredients, these loose instructions are replicable in different places around the region. Photographs represent one possible formal execution of that recipe, while sketches show various possiblities explored during design and construction.

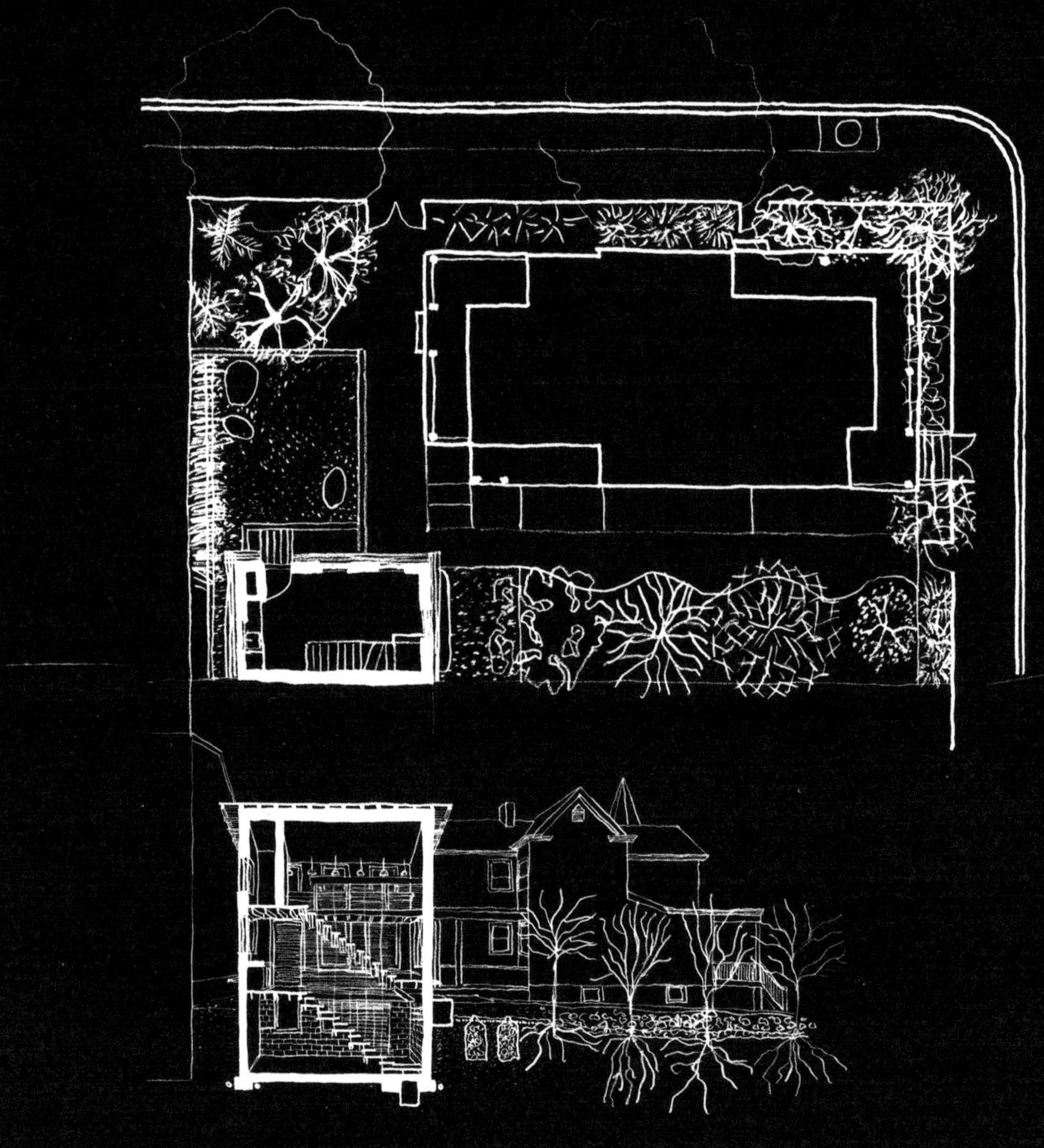

GRASS HOUSE

Anacostia, Washington, DC

On an unused parking slab behind an old house
in a historic district, gather:

1 precut BamCore kit
Equal parts BamCore to sheep's wool insulation
1 truckbed carbonized cedar siding
1 truckbed carbonized cypress siding
1 truckbed black locust sticks (still green)
1 truckbed bamboo and cork flooring
1 stack weavecore panels
1 front door - 2 parts cedar : 1 part douglas fir : 1 part cork
2 tons Omni Block masonry units
8 mycelium lamps
11 double-pane awning windows
12 bundles mixed-color willow reeds
Bronze fixtures, handles, and pulls
Copper and ceramic sinks
Dash of copper roof accessories

---

1. Assemble, stuff, and dress BamCore panels, sprinkling copper roofing nails throughout.

2. Top with slate and copper.

3. Weave willow wall to taste.

4. Frame windows in exterior siding.

5. Clad kitchen cabinets in bamboo flooring.

6. Caramelize interior walls as desired.

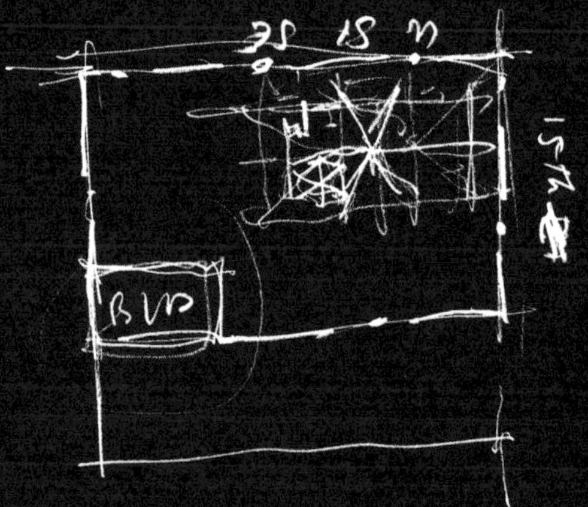
BVD

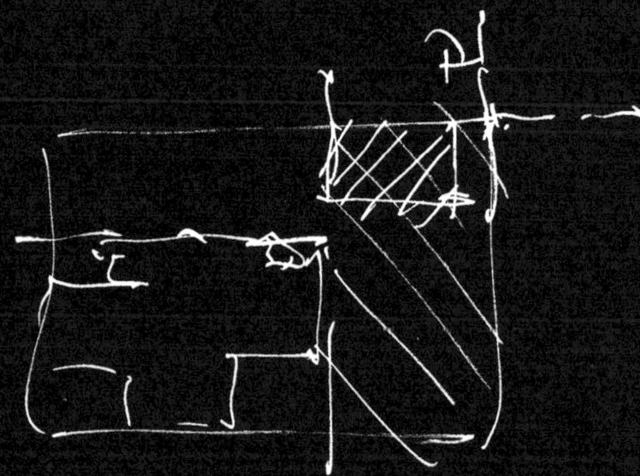

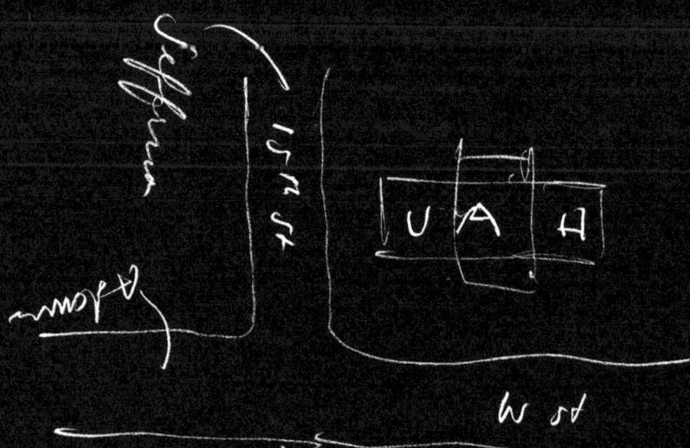
U A H
W st

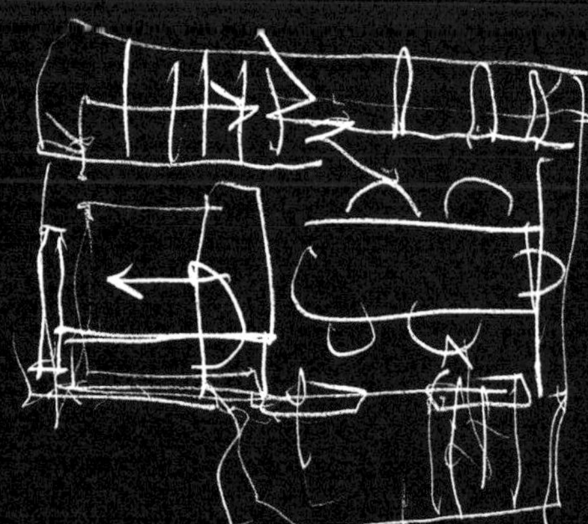

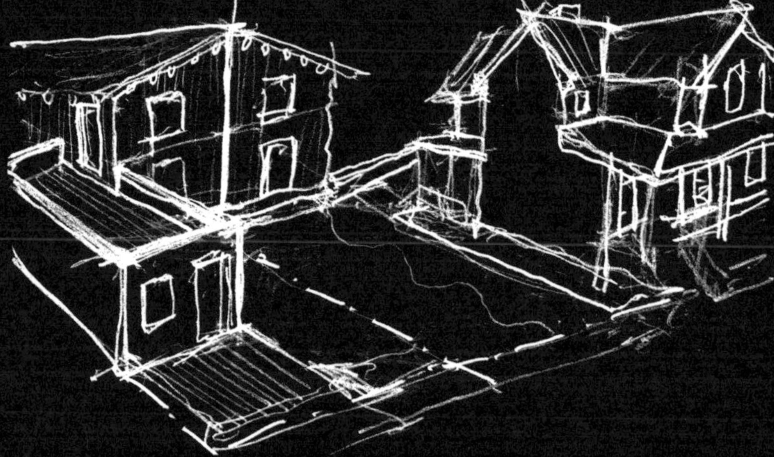

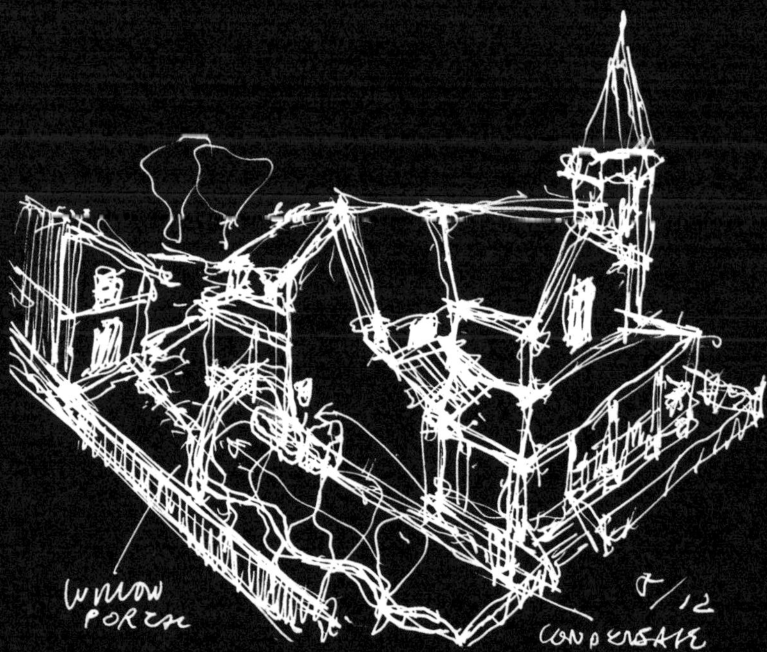
WILLOW PORCH
8/12
CONDENSATE

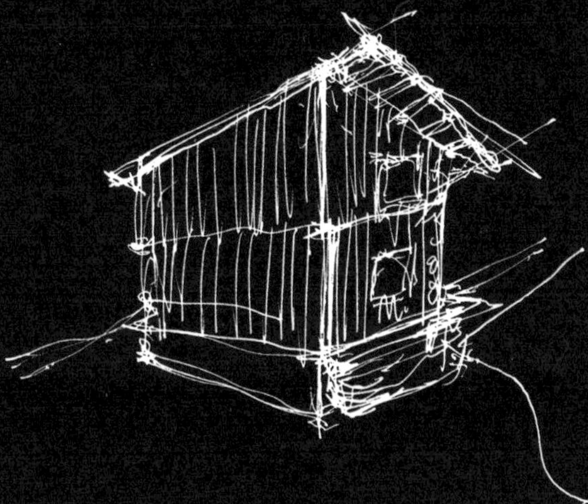

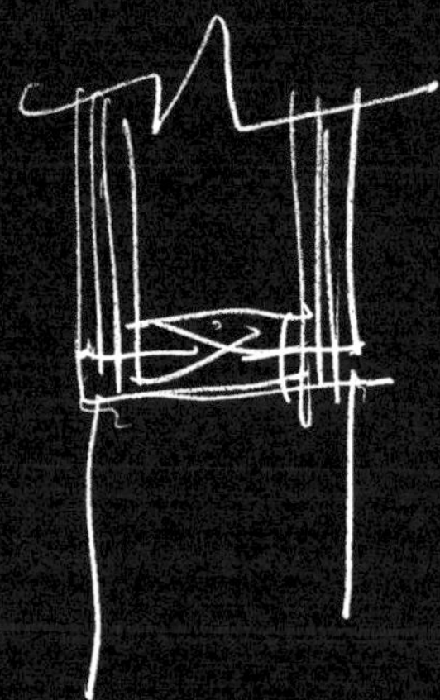

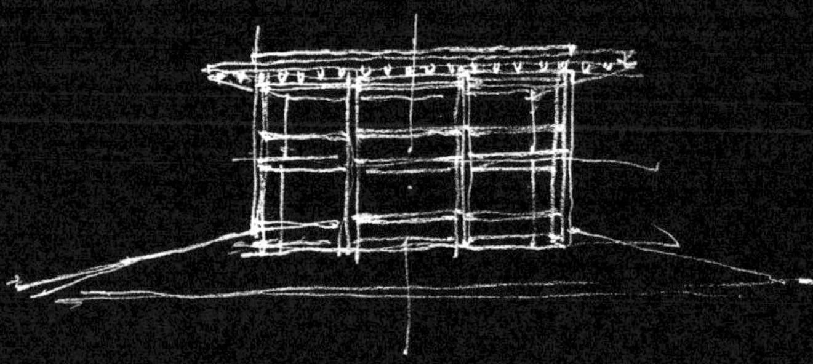

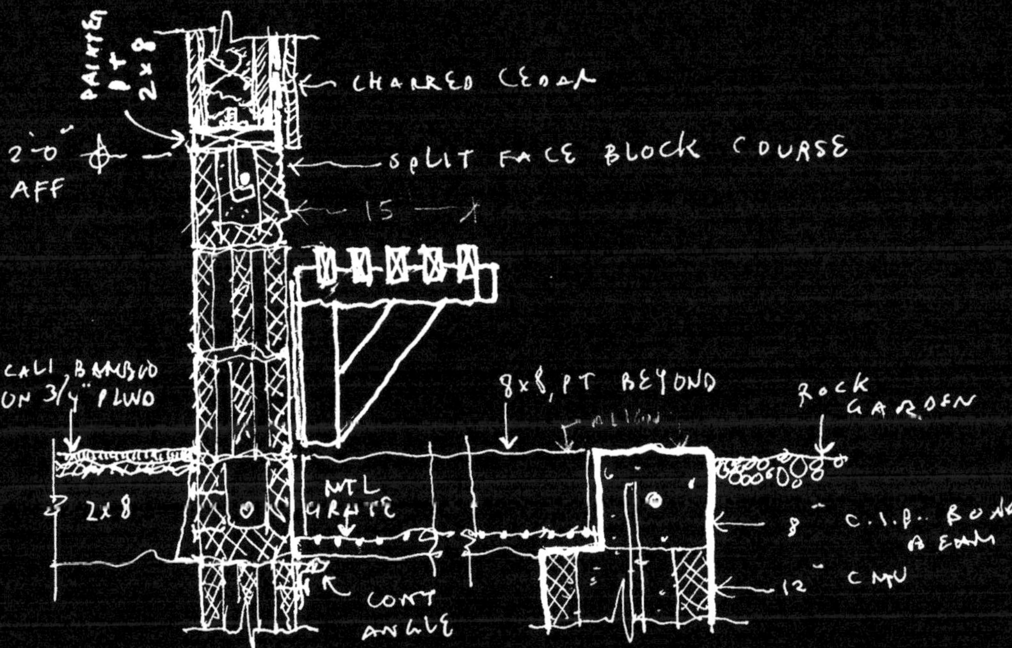
PAINTED PT 2x8
CHARRED CEDAR
2'-0" AFF
SPLIT FACE BLOCK COURSE
15
CALI BAMBOO ON 3/4" PLWD
8x8 PT BEYOND
ROCK GARDEN
MTL GRATE
2x8
8" C.I.P. BOND BEAM
12" CMU
CONT ANGLE

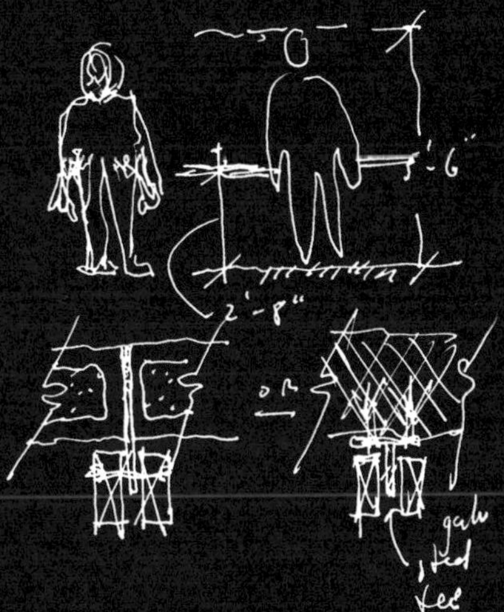
3'-6"
2'-8"
OR

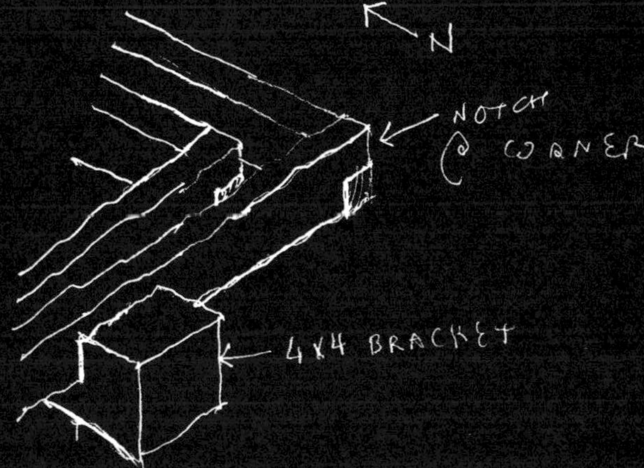
N
NOTCH
@ CORNER
4X4 BRACKET

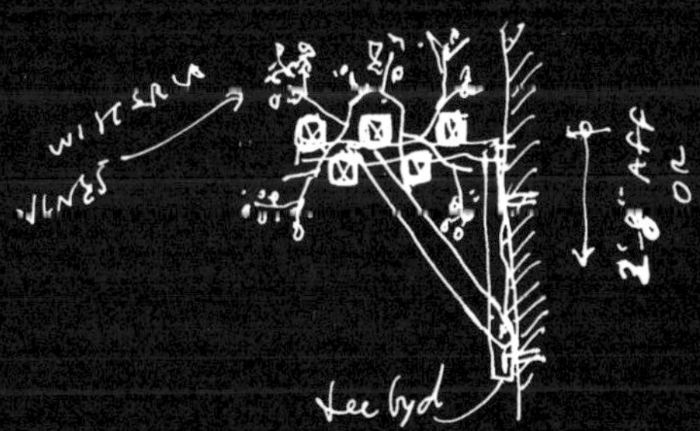
WISTERIA
VINES

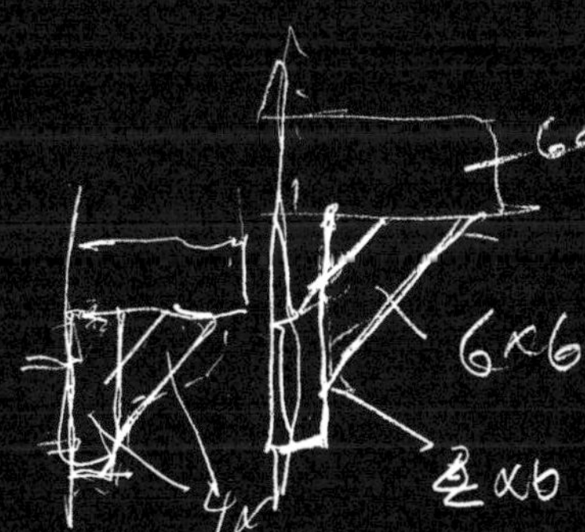
6x6
2x6

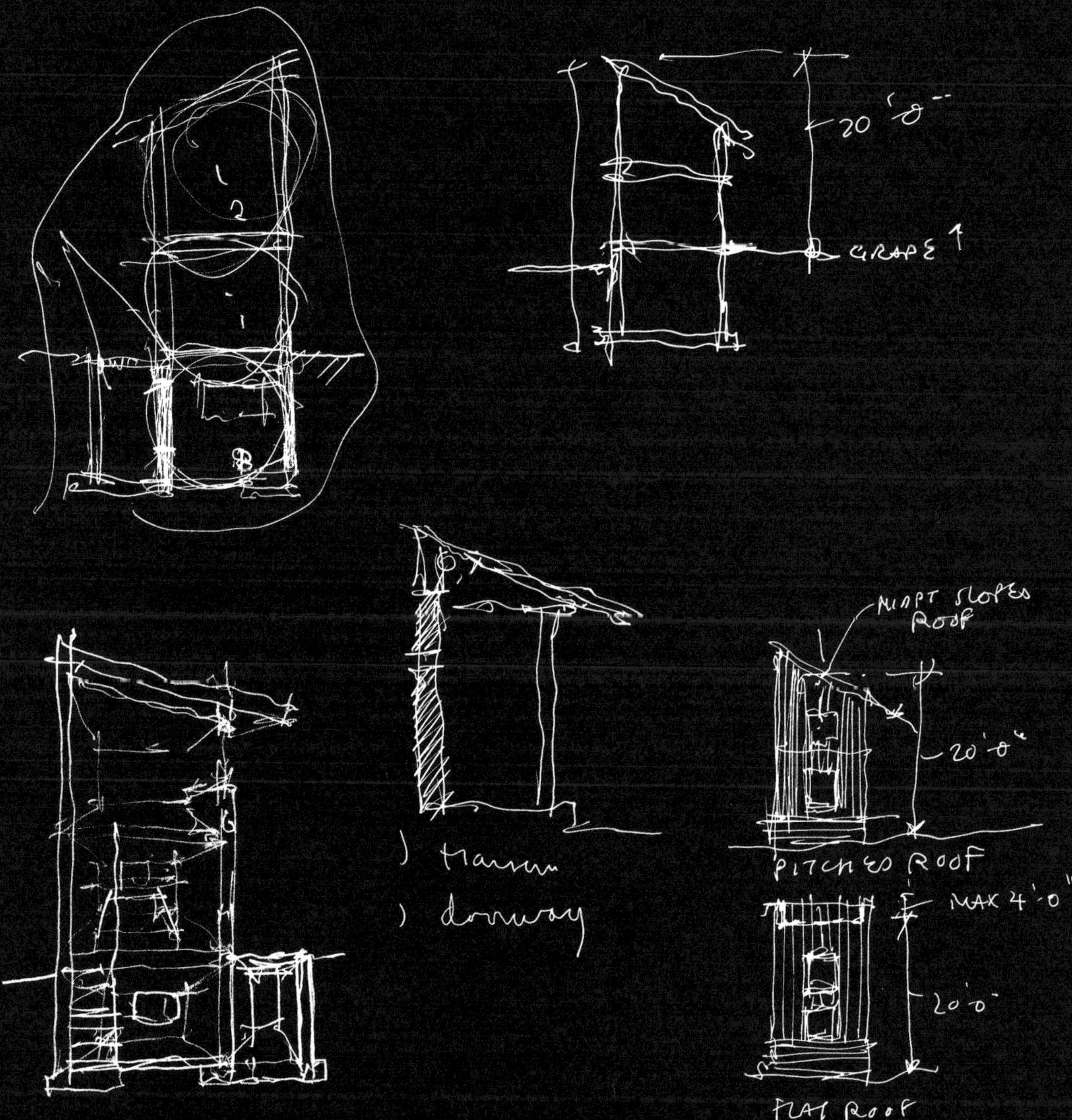
20'0"
GRADE
MIDPT SLOPED ROOF
20'0"
PITCHED ROOF
MAX 4'-0"
20'0"
FLAT ROOF
doorway

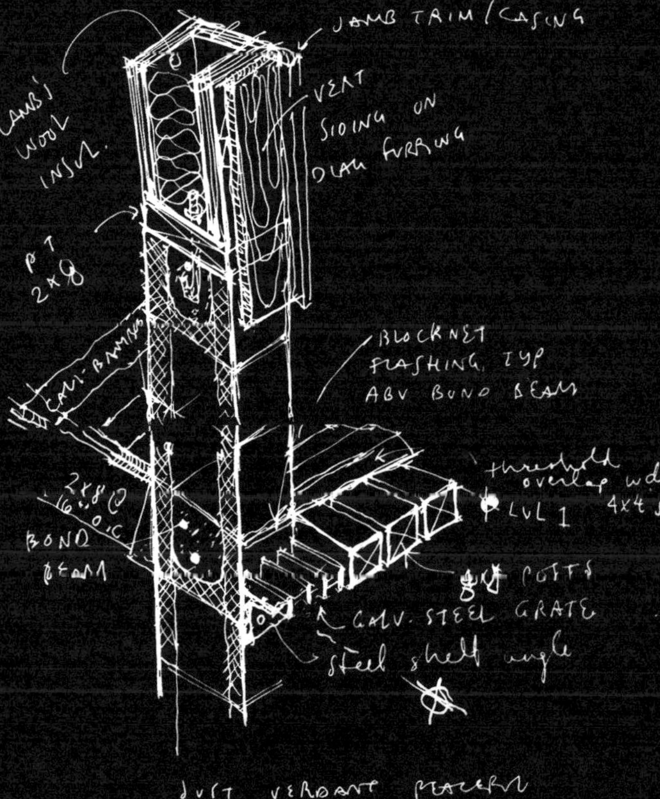
JAMB TRIM / CASING
LAMB'S WOOL INSUL.
VERT SIDING ON DIAG FURRING
PT 2x8
BLOCKNET FLASHING, TYP ABV BOND BEAM
threshold overlap wd 4x4's
LVL 1
BOND BEAM
GALV. STEEL GRATE
steel shelf angle

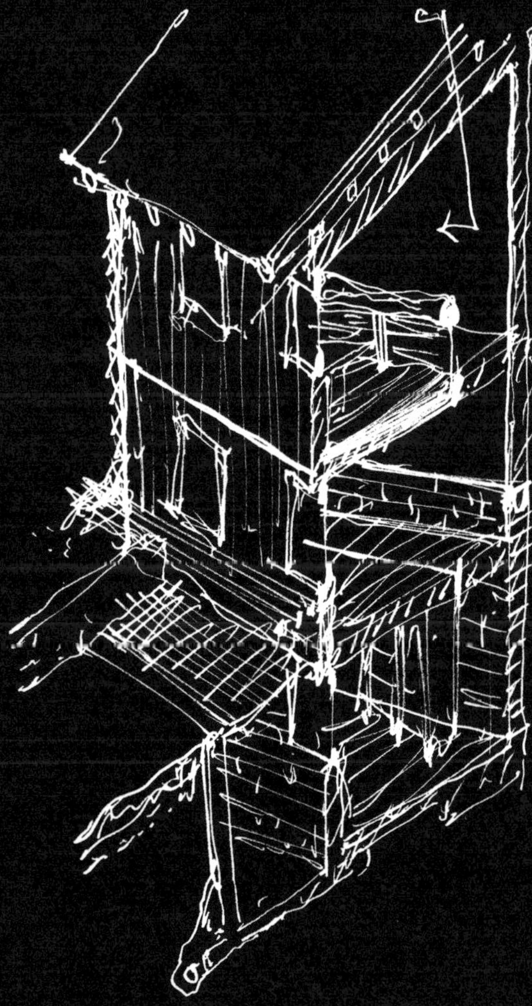

LITTLE NEMO
THE IDEA OF LOUIS SULLIVAN
New Vernacular Architecture
GRAPHIC STANDARDS
CREATING CAPITOL HILL
TAO TE CHING
THE PHILOSOPHY OF SUSTAINABLE DESIGN
S,M,L,XL
Victorian Cottage Residences
Villas and Cottages
UNBUILT
LOUIS KAHN essential texts
TOWARDS A NEW ARCHITECTURE
Bill Bryson At Home
HOME
THE TEN BOOKS ON ARCHITECTURE
THE SIXTH EXTINCTION
ELIZABETH KOLBERT
AFTER THE MAP
WILLIAM RANKIN
Anacostia
The Chesapeake: An Environmental Biography
Maryland's Eastern Shore
THE EMPTY OCEAN
A CLEARING IN THE DISTANCE
BEING AND TIME
MARTIN HEIDEGGER
THE COTTON KINGDOM
FREDERICK LAW OLMSTED
THE POWER BROKER
THE TESTAMENT OF STONE
WALDEN
THE IRON HEEL
SARTOR RESARTUS
The I CHING or Book of Changes
MY BONDAGE and MY FREEDOM
MAN'S THREE MILLION YEAR ODYSSEY
Bow-Wow from POST BUBBLE CITY
Home
KINDERGARTEN CHATS
DEMOCRACY
BUBBLES
oppenheimer

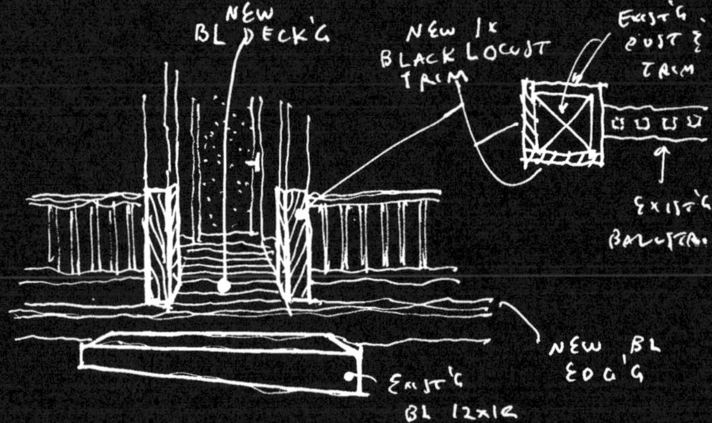
NEW BL DECK'G
NEW 1x BLACK LOCUST TRIM
EXIST'G POST & TRIM
EXIST'G BALUSTR
NEW BL EDG'G
EXIST'G BL 12x12

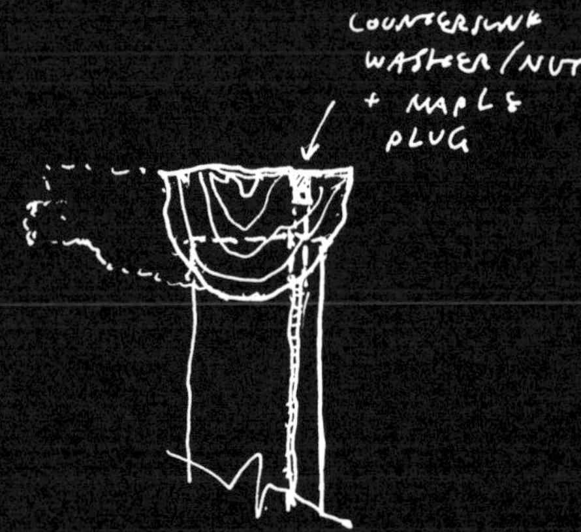
COUNTERSUNK WASHER/NUT + MAPLE PLUG

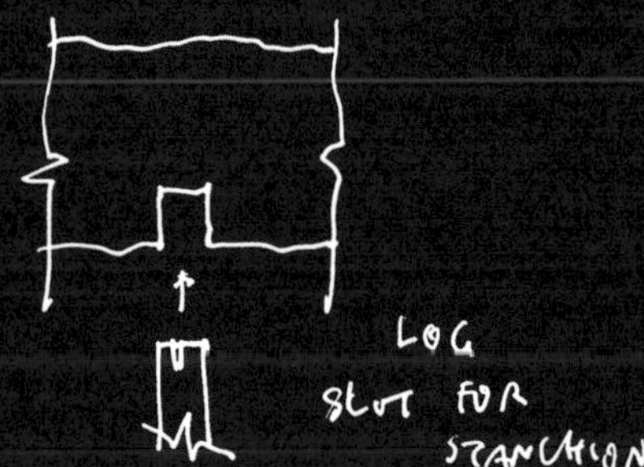
LOG
SLOT FOR STANCHION

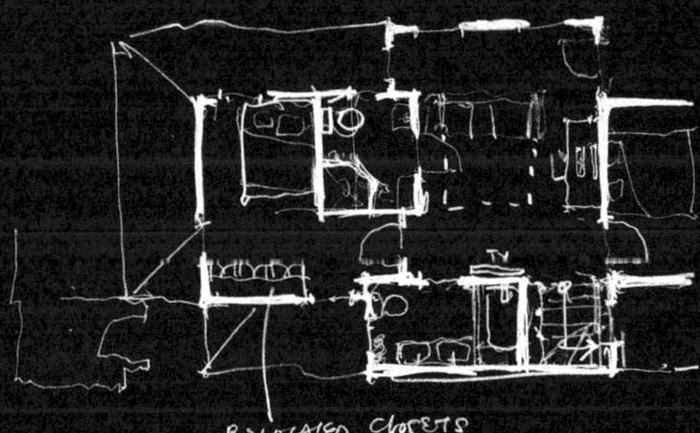
TV
RELOCATED CLOSETS

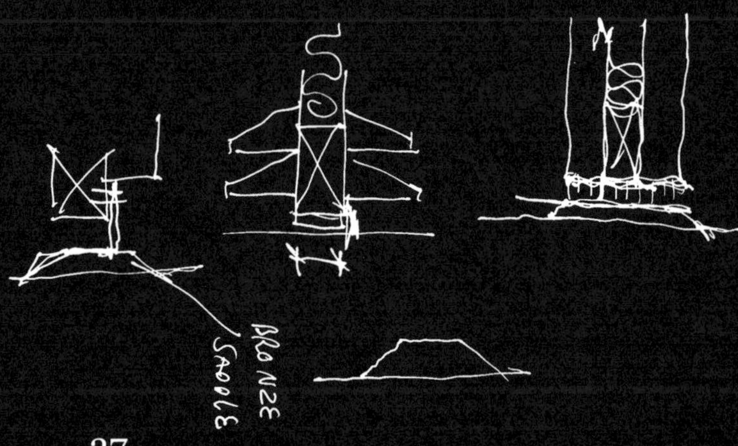
BRONZE SADDLE

SLATE

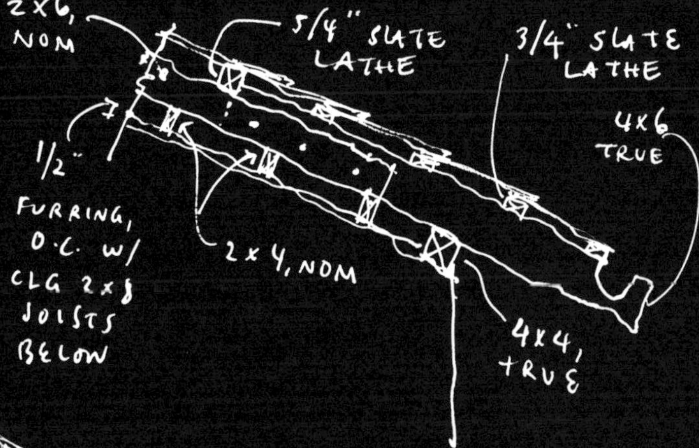
2X6, NOM
5/4" SLATE LATHE
3/4" SLATE LATHE
4X6 TRUE
1/2" FURRING, O.C. W/ CLG 2X8 JOISTS BELOW
2X4, NOM
4X4, TRUE

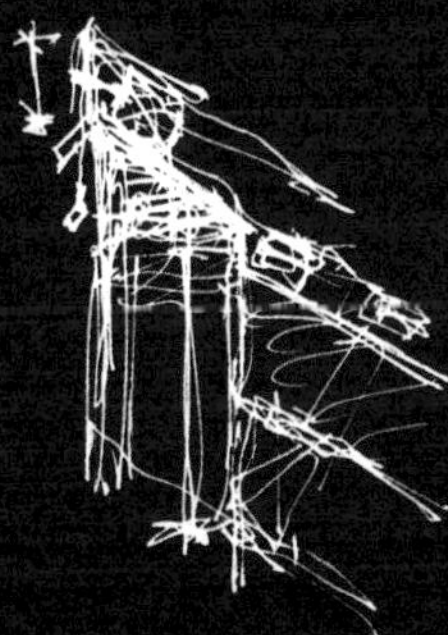

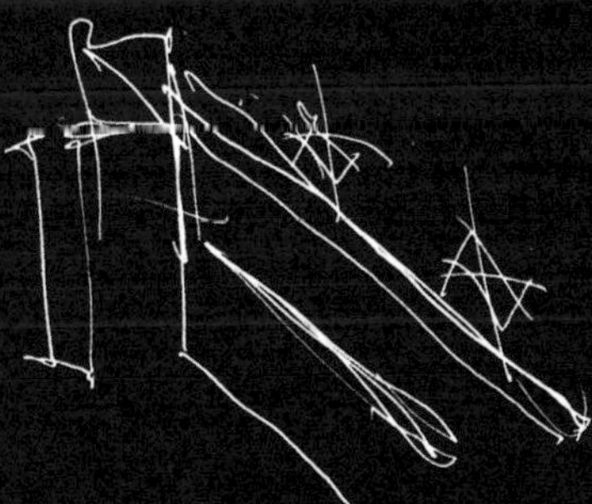

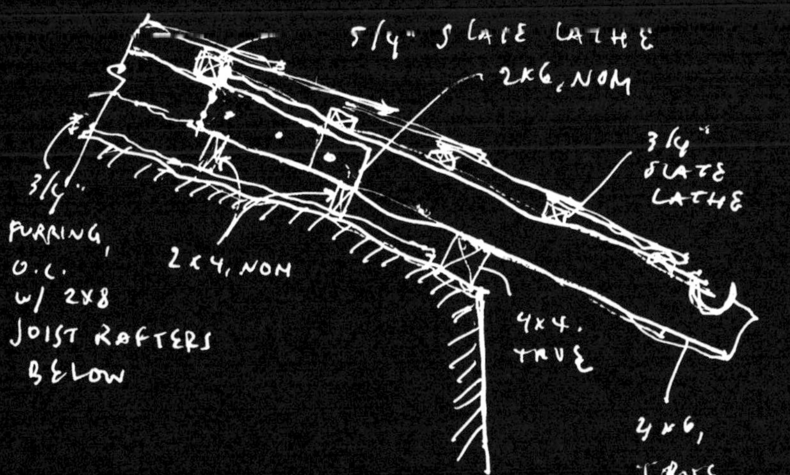
5/4" SLATE LATHE
2X6, NOM
3/4" SLATE LATHE
3/4" FURRING, O.C. W/ 2X8 JOIST RAFTERS BELOW
2X4, NOM
4X4, TRUE
4X6, TRUE

STICK HOUSE

Long Island, NY

At the back of a suburban house with a pool, gather:

(4) 4x12 beams
Equal parts 2x4s : 2x12s : 4x6s : cedar shingles : 1x6 T&G
Sprinkling of 2x2s
Sprinkling of 1x2s
1 skylight
1 ventless fireplace
1 grill
½ ton CMU blocks
Dash of copper roof accessories

---

1. Shape masonry fireplace & grill station.

2. Chop and stand 2x4 studs.

3. Lift 4x12s into place.

4. Anchor to existing house with 4x6 ledgers; top with skylight.

5. Crown with 2x12s; cover with 1x6 T&G boards and cedar shingles; finish roof with copper.

6. Stretch pet-grade screening over studding; match each interior 2x4 with an exterior 1x2 strip.

7. Assemble perimeter 1x6 T&G board bench and shelf. Add (2) doors of 2x2 / 2x12 sticks.

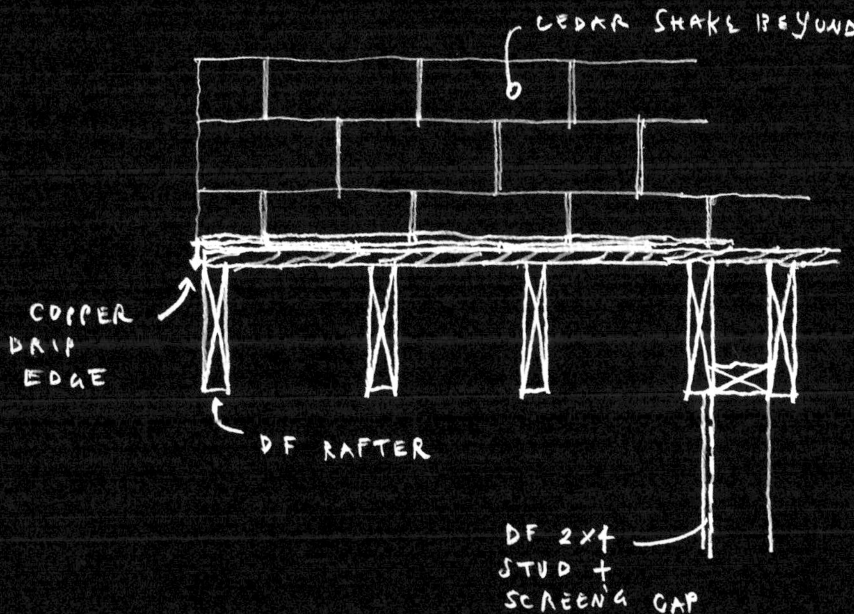
CEDAR SHAKE BEYOND
COPPER
DRIP
EDGE
DF RAFTER
DF 2X4
STUD +
SCREENING GAP

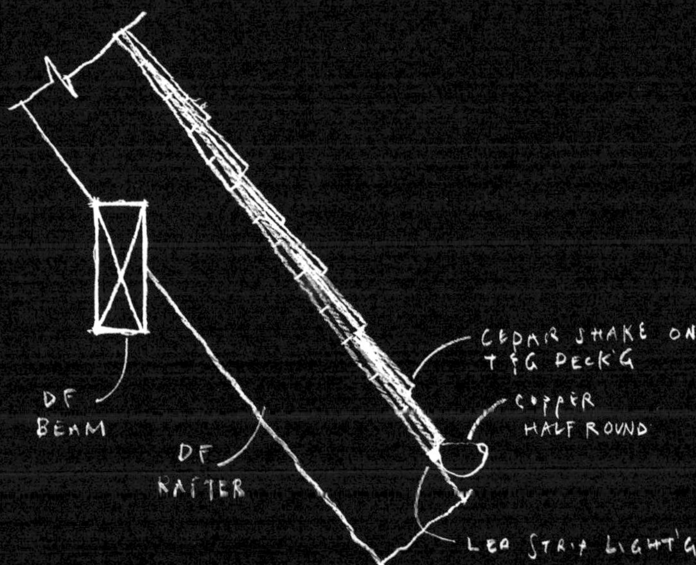
CEDAR SHAKE ON
T & G DECK'G
COPPER
HALF ROUND
DF
BEAM
DF
RAFTER
LED STRIP LIGHT'G

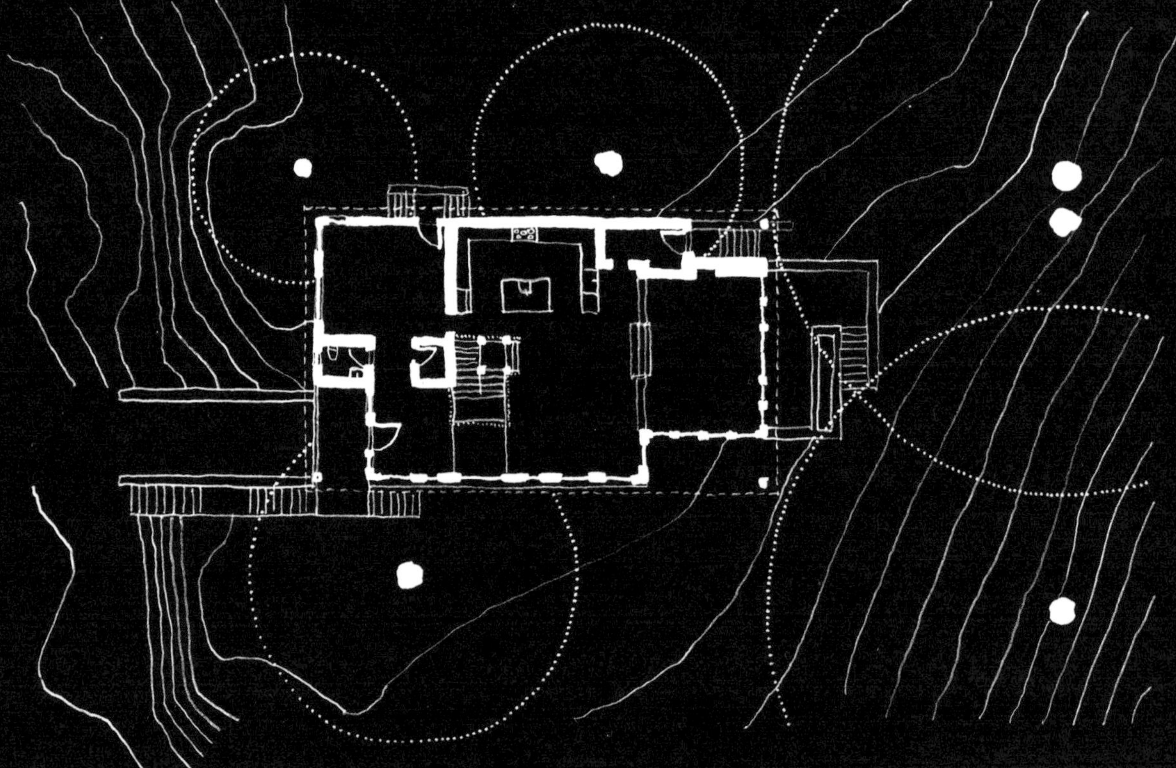

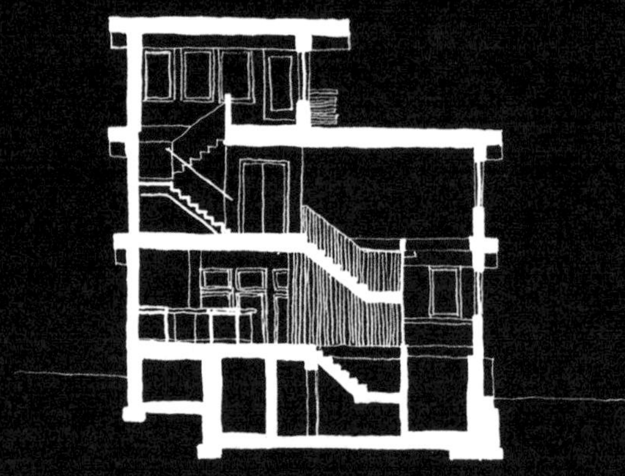

POPLAR CLOUD

Palisades, Washington, DC

On an existing sensitive foundation surrounded
by mature, forested parkland, gather:

A large heap of studs
Too much steel
Equal parts BamCore to sheep's wool insulation
Siding - 1 part caramelized cork : 1 part bark : 1 part cypress
Large cypress beams as needed
Concrete foundation reinforcement
Carpet sedum
7 doors
64 wooden windows
Strips of copper flashing

---

1. Level existing stick-frame house, leaving intact foundation to avoid disturbing the surrounding trees' roots.

2. Frame house with wood studs using steel beams where needed to create large interior spaces.

3. Dress in siding, alternating materials from one horizontal layer to the next. Pipe copper flashing between layers.

4. Garnish with sedum carpets.

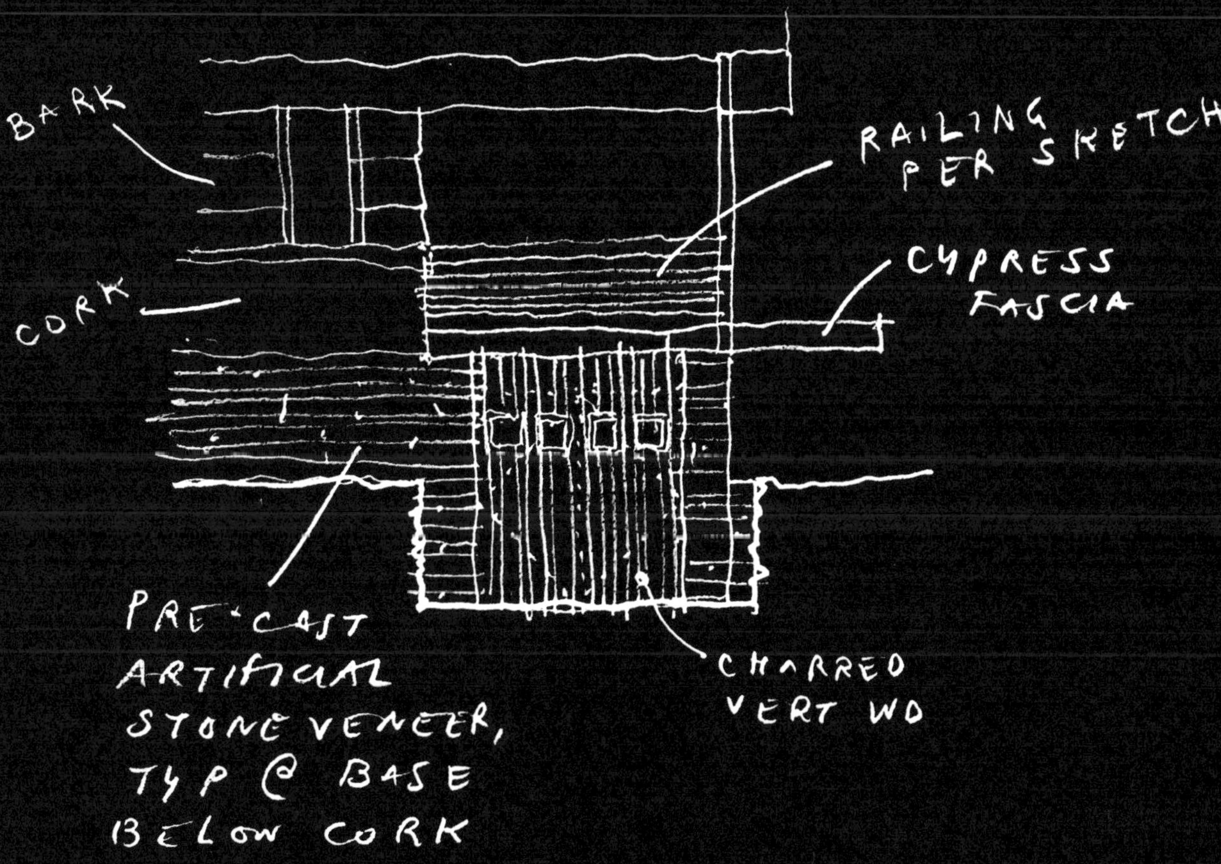
BARK
RAILING PER SKETCH
CYPRESS FASCIA
CORK
PRE-CAST ARTIFICIAL STONE VENEER, TYP @ BASE BELOW CORK
CHARRED VERT WD

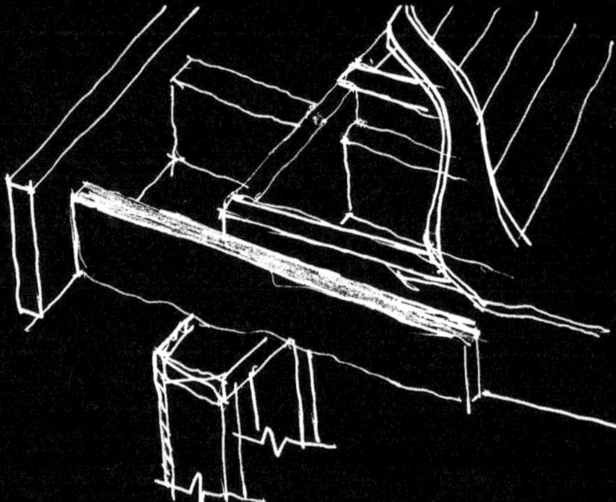

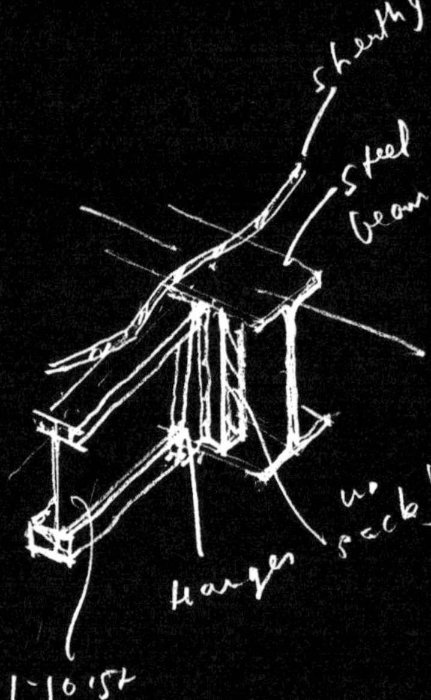
sheathg
steel beam
hanger
I-joist

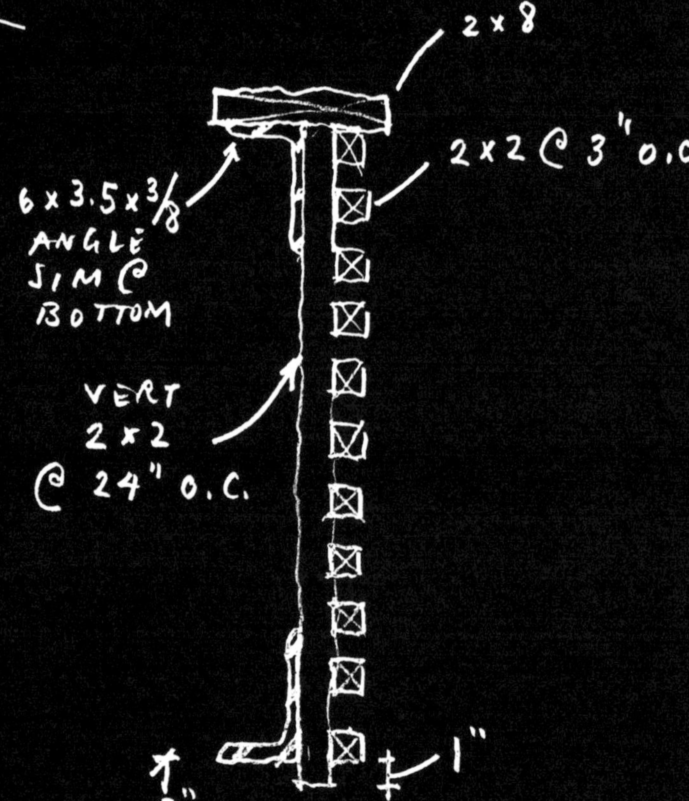
2 x 8
2 x 2 @ 3" O.C
6 x 3.5 x 3/8 ANGLE SIM @ BOTTOM
VERT 2 x 2 @ 24" O.C.
1"
3"

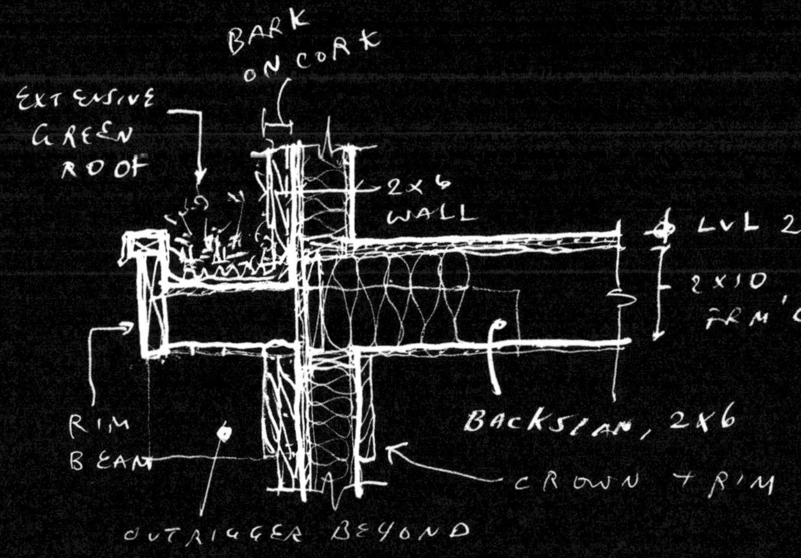
BARK
ON CORK
EXTENSIVE
GREEN
ROOF
2x6
WALL
LVL 2
2x10
FRM'G
RIM
BEAM
BACKSPAN, 2x6
CROWN + RIM
OUTRIGGER BEYOND

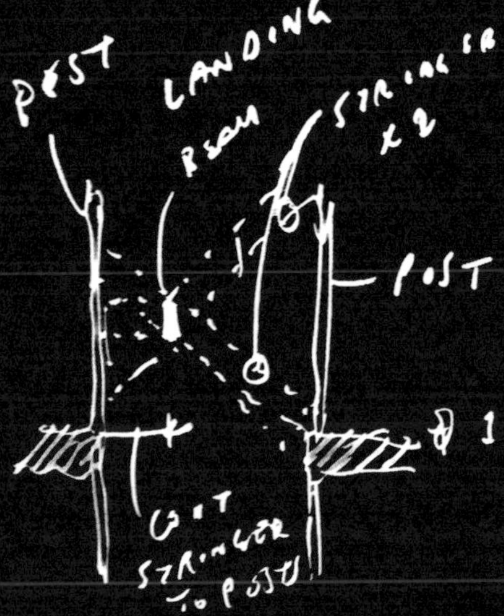
POST
LANDING
BEAM
STRINGER
x 2
POST
STRINGER
TO POSTS

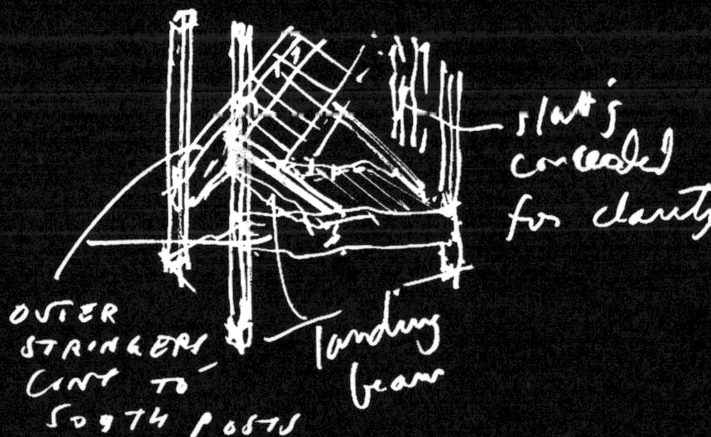
slats
concealed
for clarity
OUTER
STRINGERS
TO
SOUTH POSTS
landing
beam

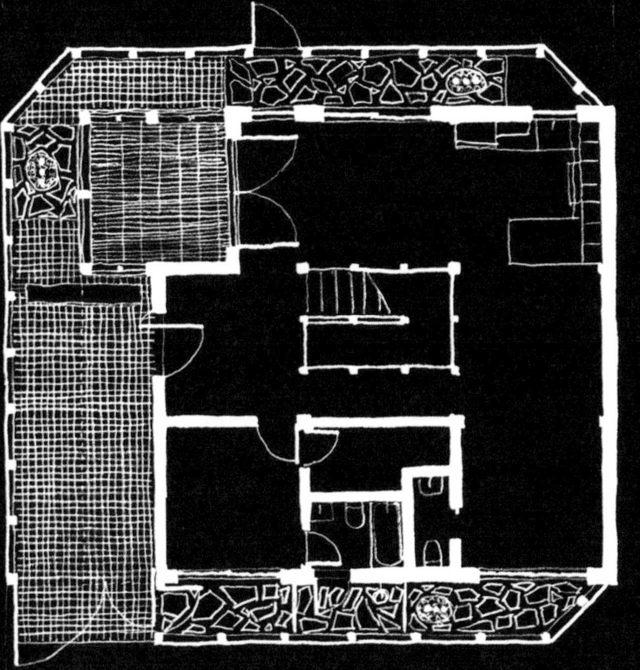

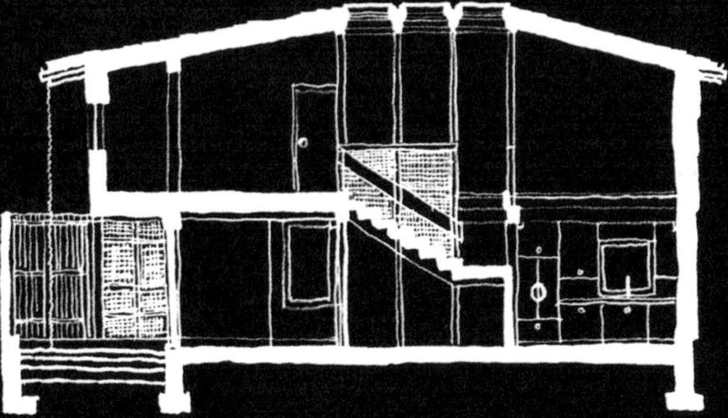

POPLAR GROVE

Adelaide Alley, Washington, DC

In an alley near a cemetery and river, gather:

1 precut BamCore kit with sheep's wool insulation
Bundles of douglas fir 2x12s
Generous helpings of interior plywood
Tulip poplar posts, hewn as required
16 parts cork : 4 parts bark : 2 parts sassafras : 1 part oak
1 truckbed sassafras fence boards
1 truckbed accoya pine roof shingles
1 truckbed salvaged Tennessee Pink Marble
1 front door - 1 part oak : 1 part cypress : 1 part poplar
5 sliding glass doors, 7 Triple pane windows, and 10 Skylights
10 tubs milk paint
Copper roof guttering and rain chains
Brass fixtures, handles, pulls, and sinks
1 bundle of mesh net : 1 bundle of pet-grade screening

---

1. Fell existing mulberry tree; mill lumber; set aside.

2. Form, stuff, and dress BamCore panels. Frame screened porch and balcony with black locust and reserved mulberry logs; stretch and bind pet-grade screening across openings.

3. Lace sassafras and black locust fence along property lines. Arrange roof eaves and skylight. Top with accoya and copper.

4. Cover interior partitions with poplar plywood, BamCore interior surfaces with milk paint, and ceilings with maple plywood.

5. Assemble stair and stretch mesh net to length.

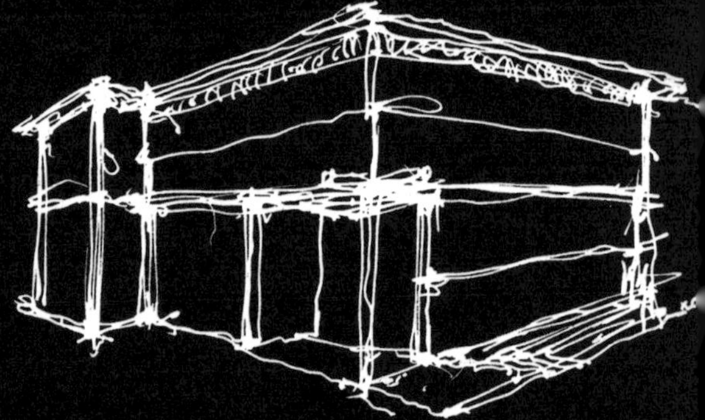
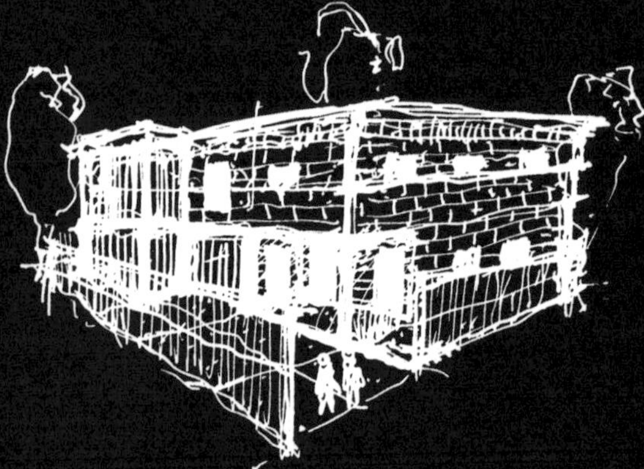
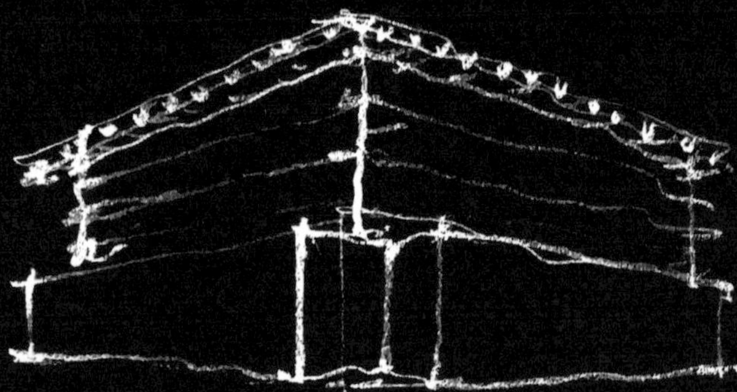
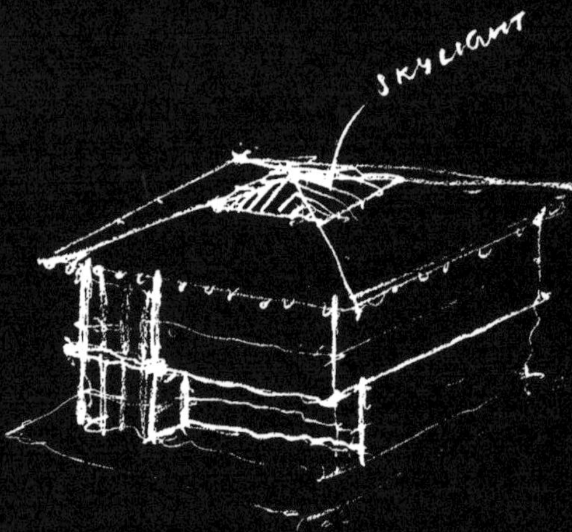
SKYLIGHT
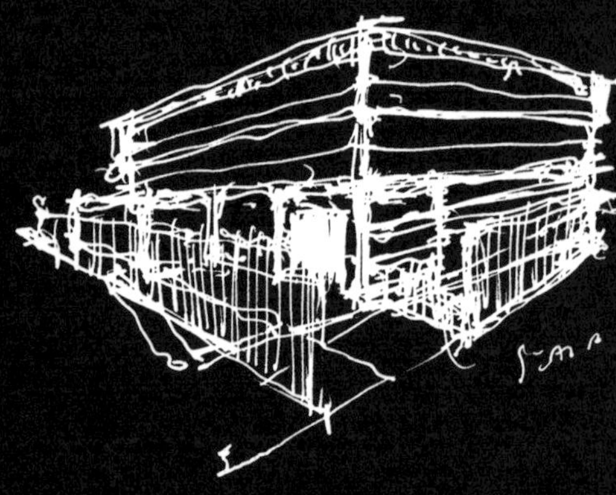

KIDS

435

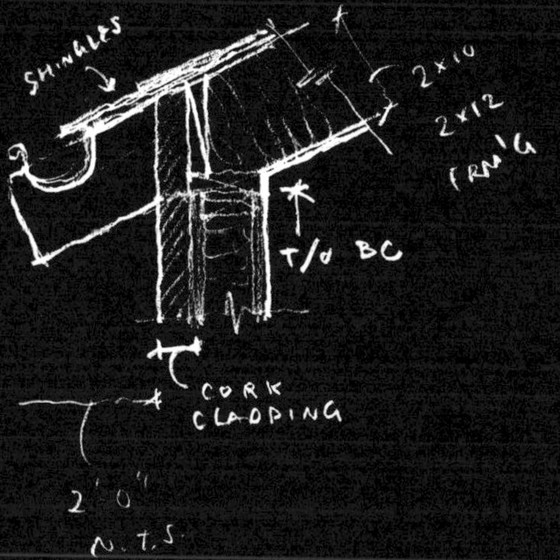
SHINGLES
2×10
2×12
FRM'G
T/O BC
CORK
CLADDING
2'-0"
N.T.S.

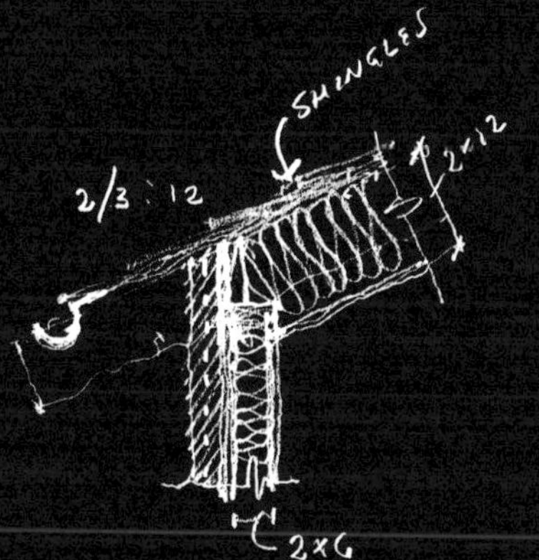
SHINGLES
2/3:12
2×12
2×6

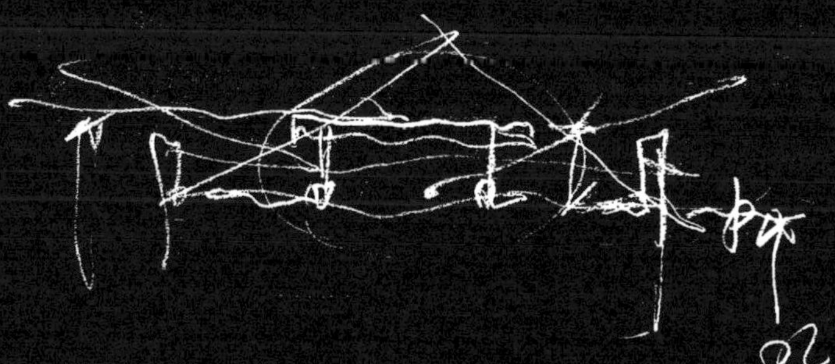

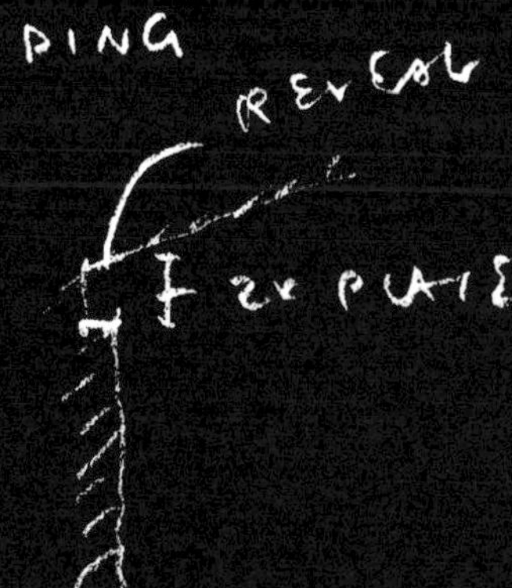
DING
REVEAL
2× PLATE

SLOPE

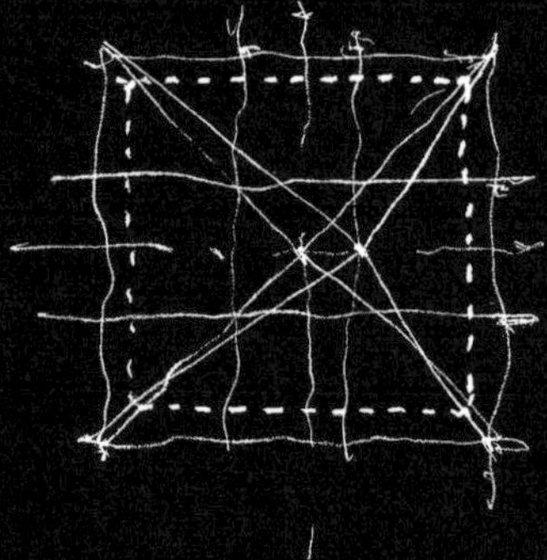

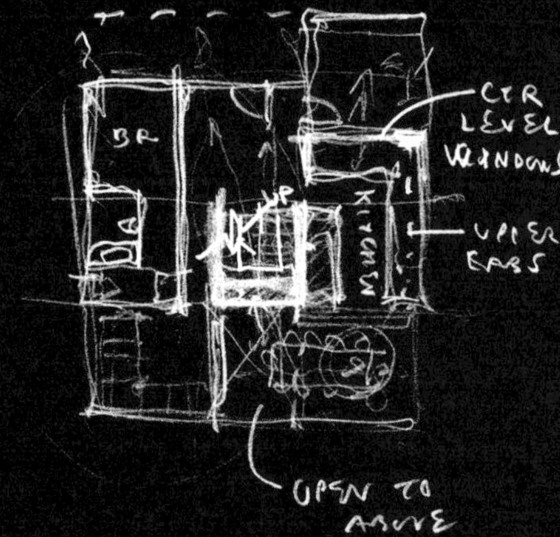
BR
UP
KITCHEN
CTR LEVEL WINDOWS
UPPER CABS
OPEN TO ABOVE

BEAM BELOW

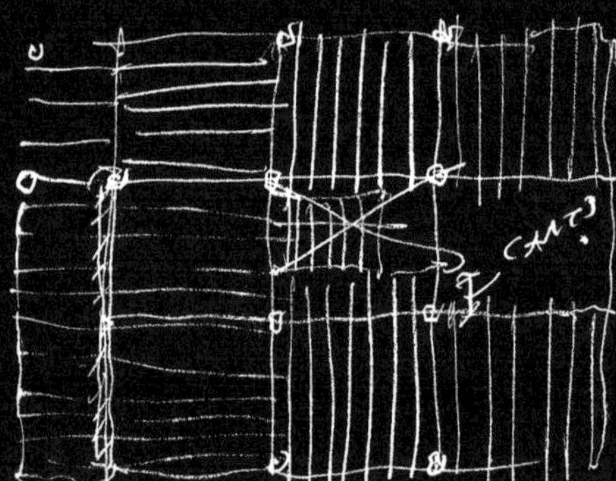

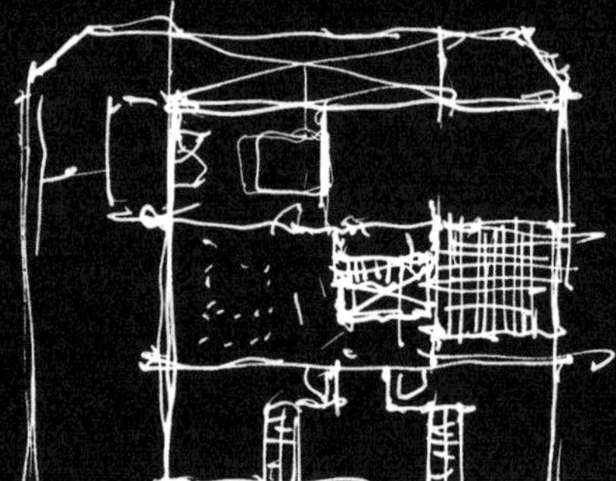

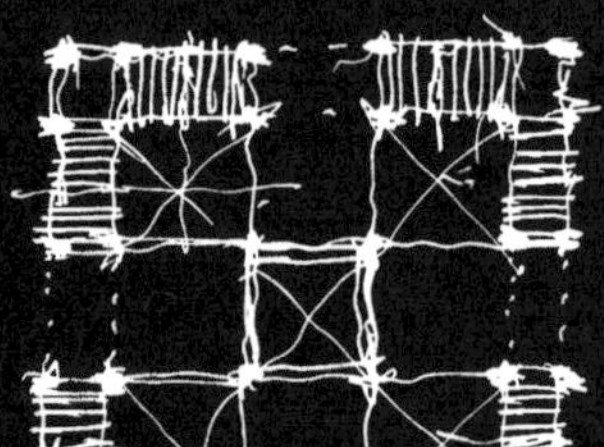

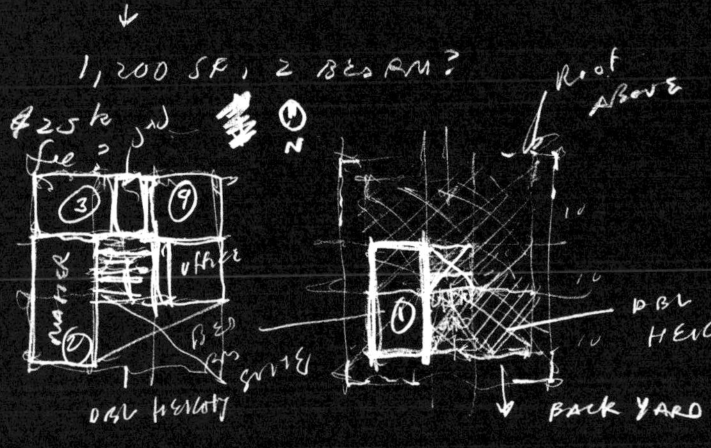
1,200 SF, 2 BEDRM?
OFFICE
MASTER
BED SUITE
DBL HEIGHT
ROOF ABOVE
DBL HEIGHT
BACK YARD
N

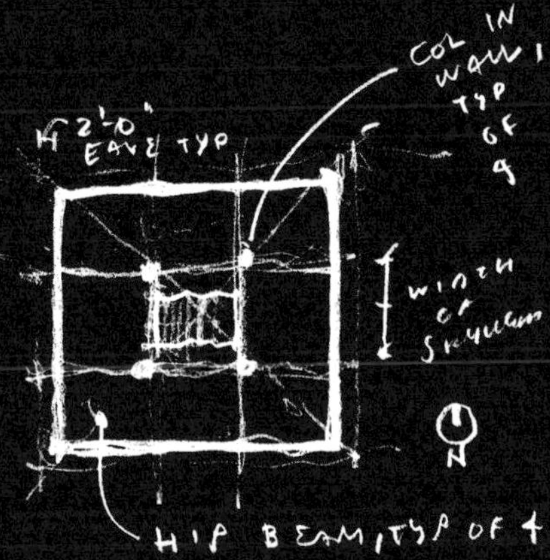
2'-0" EAVE TYP
COL IN WALL, TYP OF 4
WIDTH OF SKYLIGHT
N
HIP BEAM, TYP OF 4

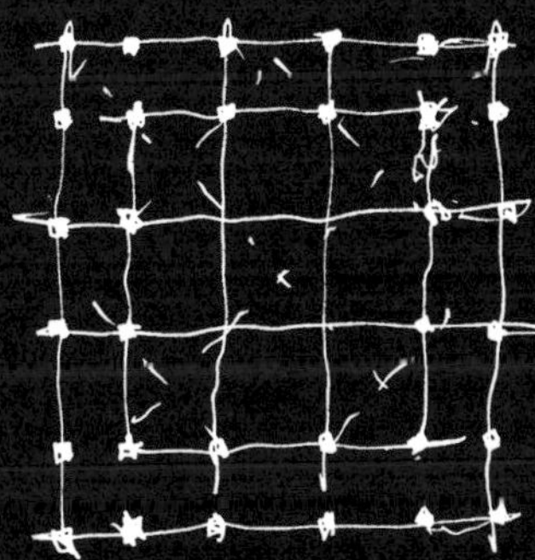

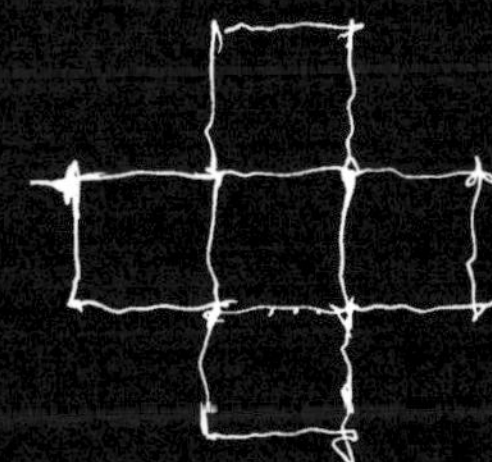

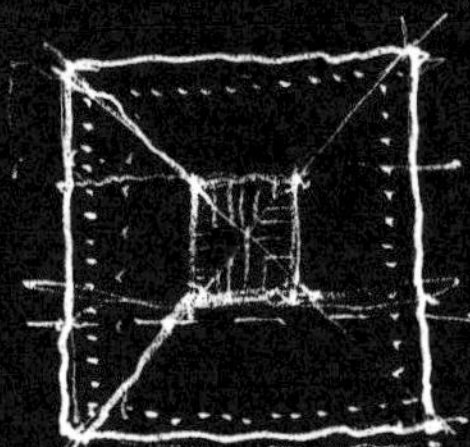

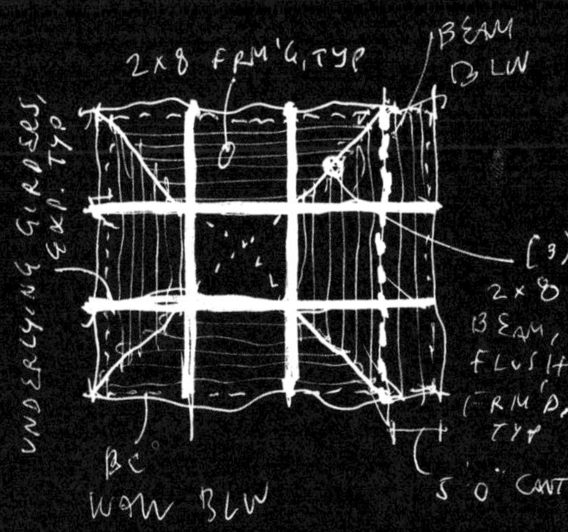
2x8 FRM'G, TYP
BEAM BLW
UNDERLYING GIRDERS, EXP. TYP
(3) 2x8 BEAM, FLUSH FRM'D, TYP
5'-0" CANT
WALL BLW

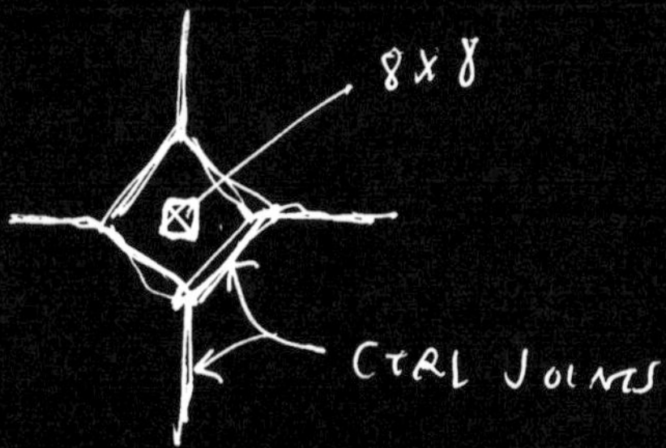
8x8
CTRL JOINTS

8x8 below

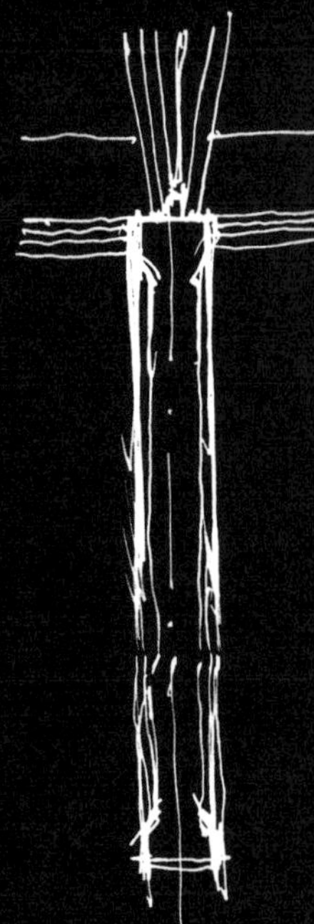

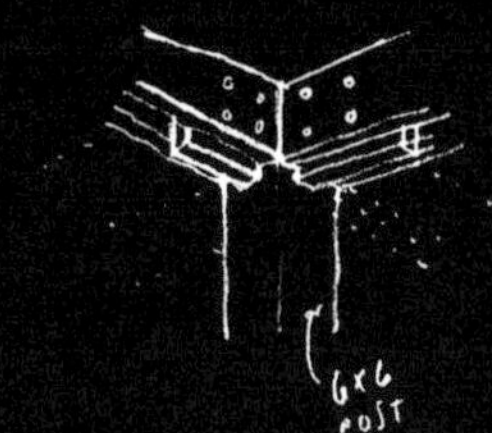
6x6
POST

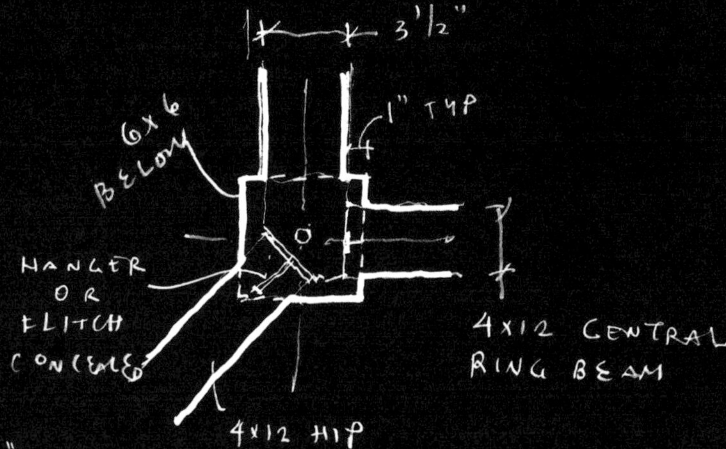
3½"
1" TYP
6x6
BELOW
HANGER
OR
FLITCH
CONCEALED
4x12 CENTRAL
RING BEAM
4x12 HIP

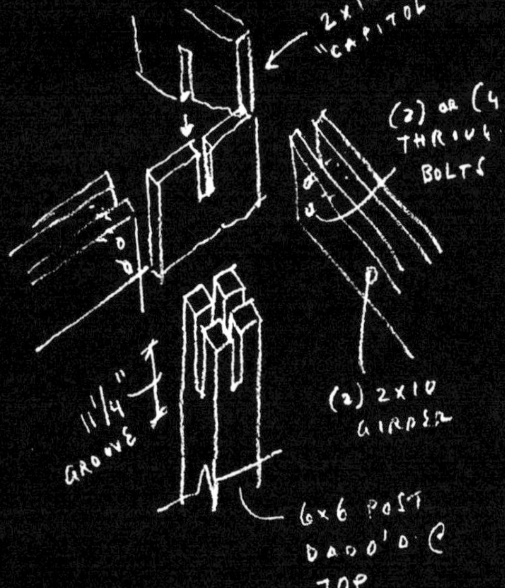
2x12
"CAPITOL"
(2) OR (4
THRU
BOLTS
1¼"
GROOVE
(2) 2x10
GIRDER
6x6 POST
DADO'D @
TOP

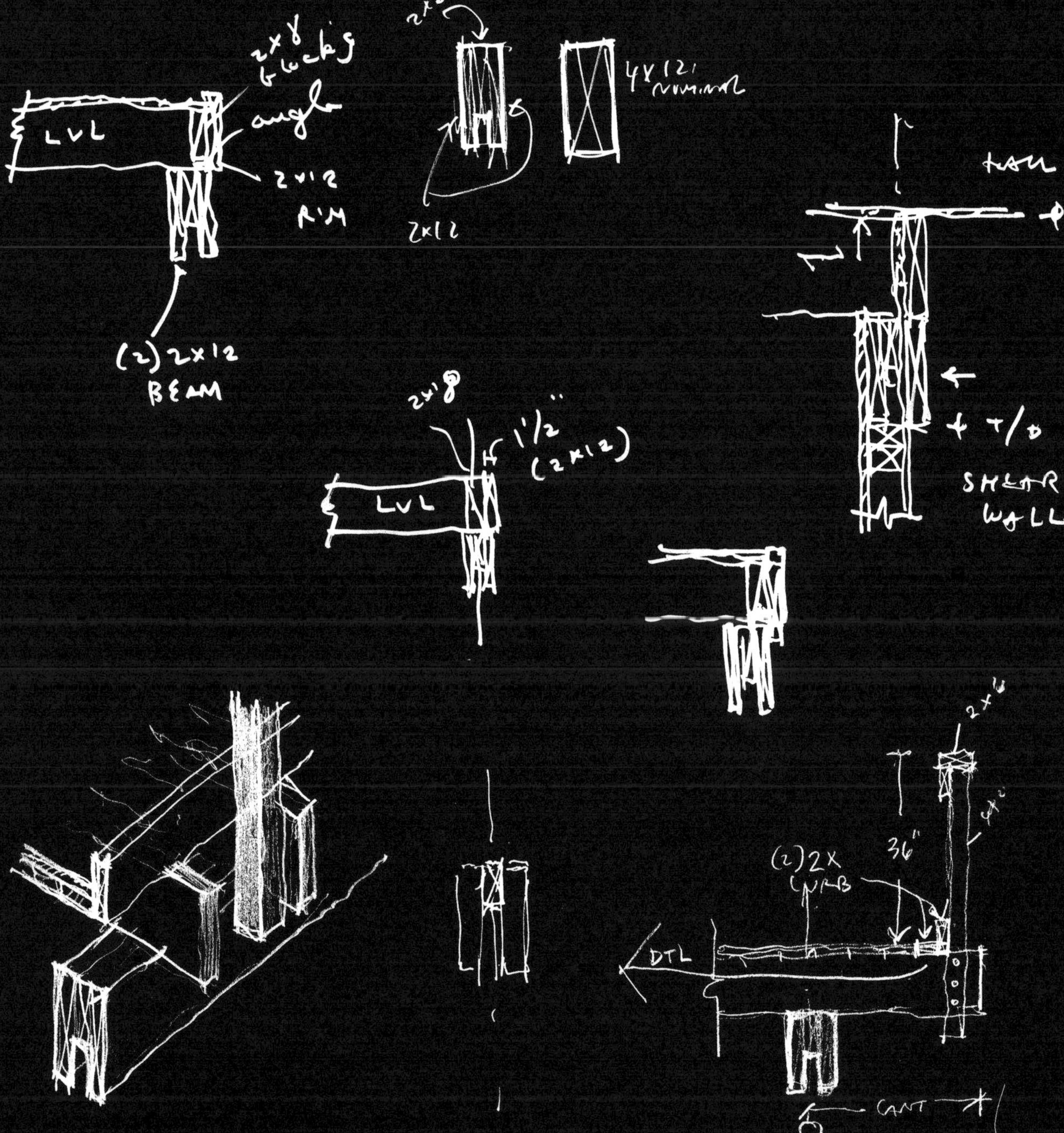
2x8 blocking
angle
LVL
2x12 RIM
(2) 2x12 BEAM
2x8
2x12
4x12 nominal
WALL
T/O
SHEAR WALL
2x8
1½" (2x12)
LVL
(2) 2X CURB
36"
DTL
CANT

TIMBERS

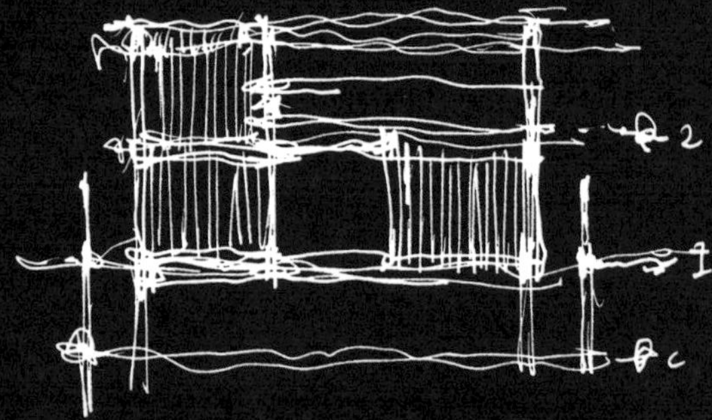

POPLAR

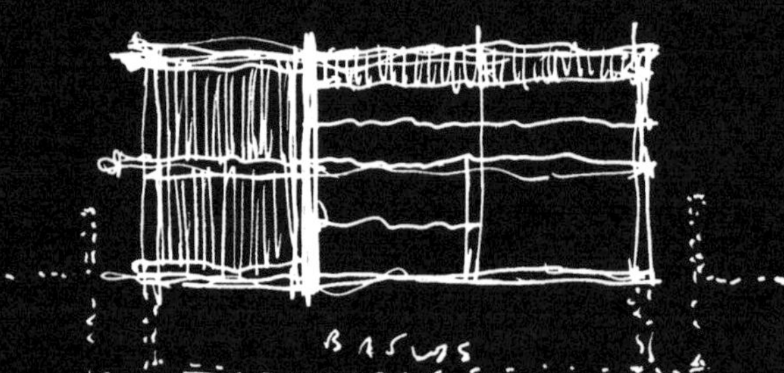
BASINS

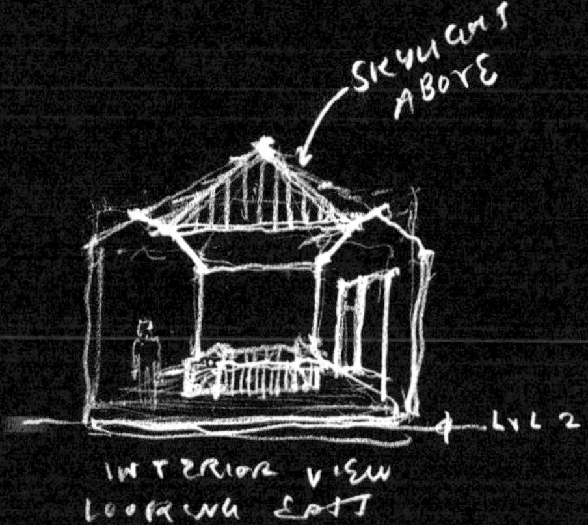
SKYLIGHTS ABOVE
LVL 2
INTERIOR VIEW LOOKING EAST

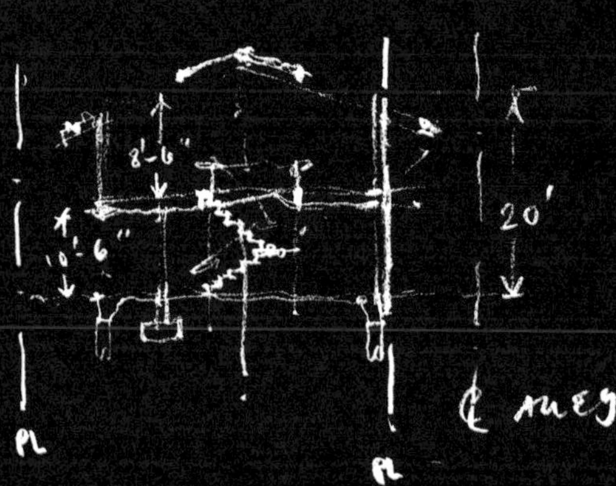
8'-6"
10'-6"
20'
℄ ALLEY
PL
PL

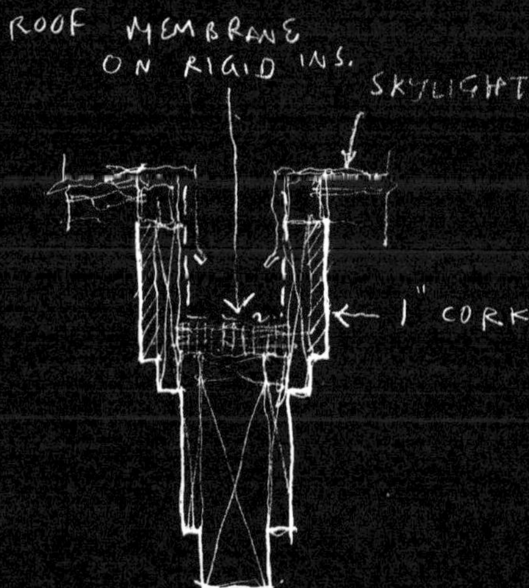
ROOF MEMBRANE ON RIGID INS.
SKYLIGHT
1" CORK

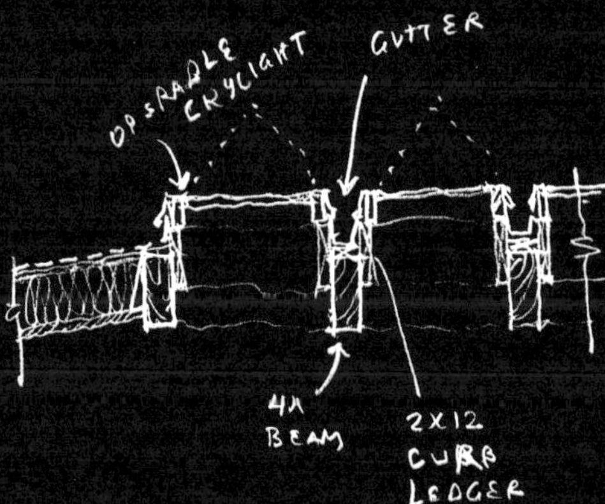
OPERABLE SKYLIGHT
GUTTER
4X BEAM
2X12 CURB LEDGER

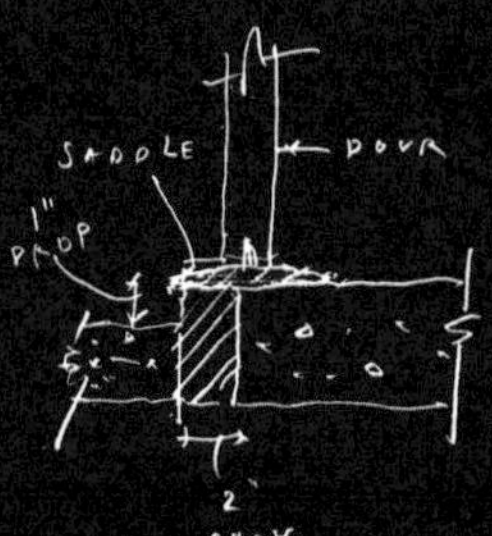
SADDLE
DOOR
1" PROP
2" CORK

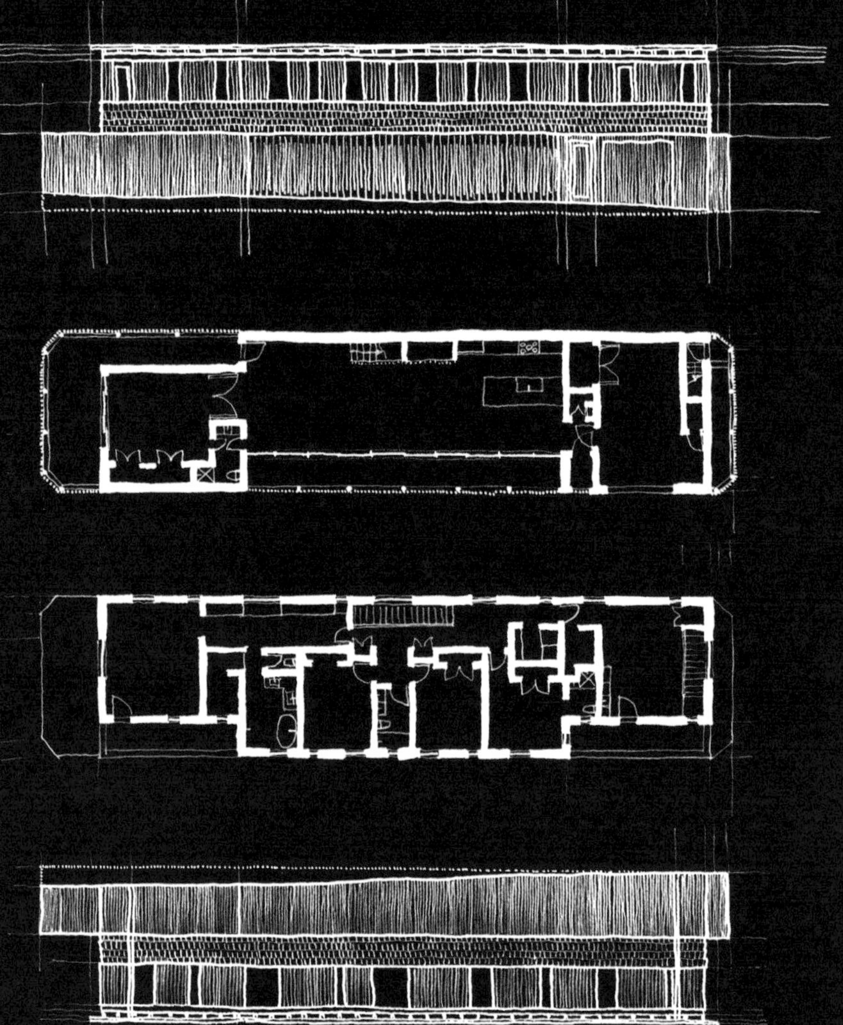

WIDE HOUSE

Lois Mailou Jones Alley, Washington, DC

On a long vacant alley lot with its wide side facing south, combine:

1 precut BamCore kit
Equal parts BamCore to cellulose insulation
Cedar beams
Pine siding - 3 parts vertical pine boards :
3 parts vertical pine fence boards :1 part cedar shingles
1 garage door
3 skylights
4 glass exterior doors
4 sliding glass doors with 5 inoperable windows
24 casement windows

---

1. Erect, fill, and dress BamCore kit, alternating between layers of cedar and pine elements.

2. Top with a roof membrane of your choice.
   Add solar panels and/or sedum carpet to taste.

3. Fold in windows, doors, and skylights.

4. Blend oak treads, risers, and balustrade into custom staircase.

5. Install kitchens and baths.

TOW AWAY
NO STANDING OR PARKING ANYTIME
ZONE 1 RESIDENT PERMIT ONLY
7AM-8:30PM
MONDAY-FRIDAY
NO PARKING
MONDAY
12:30PM TO 2:30PM
STREET SWEEPING

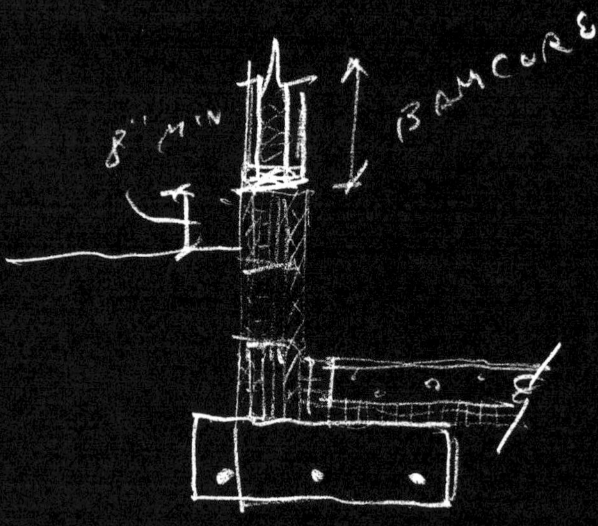

8" MIN
BAMCORE

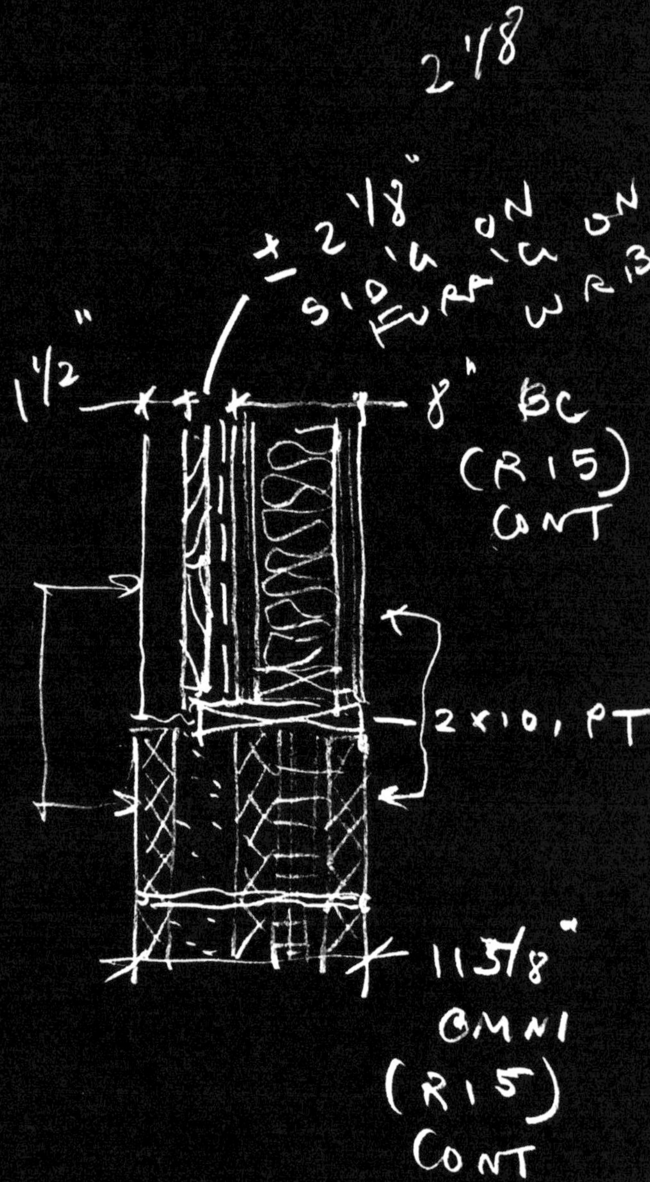

2 1/8"
± 2 1/8" SIDING ON FURRING ON WRB
1 1/2"
8" BC (R15) CONT
2×10, PT
11 5/8" OMNI (R15) CONT

2

NO DUMPING
NO PARKING IN ALLEY

1¼
WP
RAIN
SCRN
BC
2X
VERT
FENCE/
BATTENS
PT
2X
SILL
SEALER
OMNI
THERMACORK
R-5?

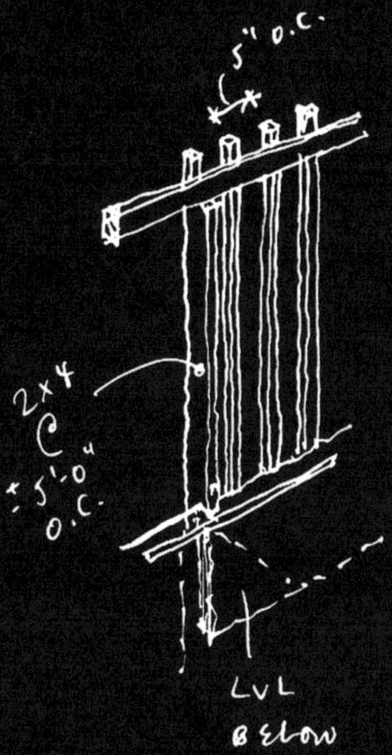
5" O.C.
2x4 @ ±5'-0" O.C.
LVL BELOW

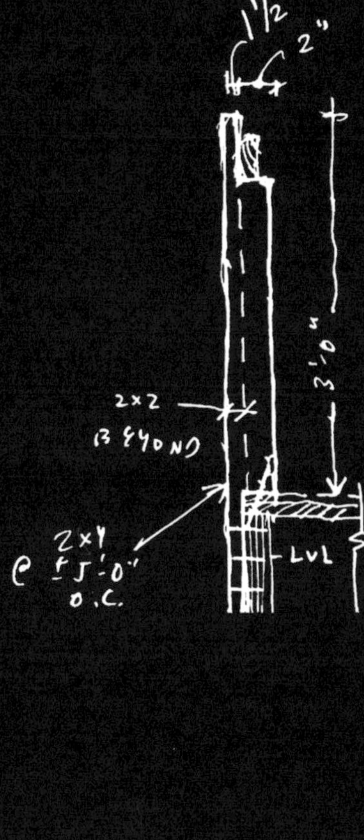
1½"
2"
3'-0"
2x2 BEYOND
2x4 @ ±5'-0" O.C.
LVL

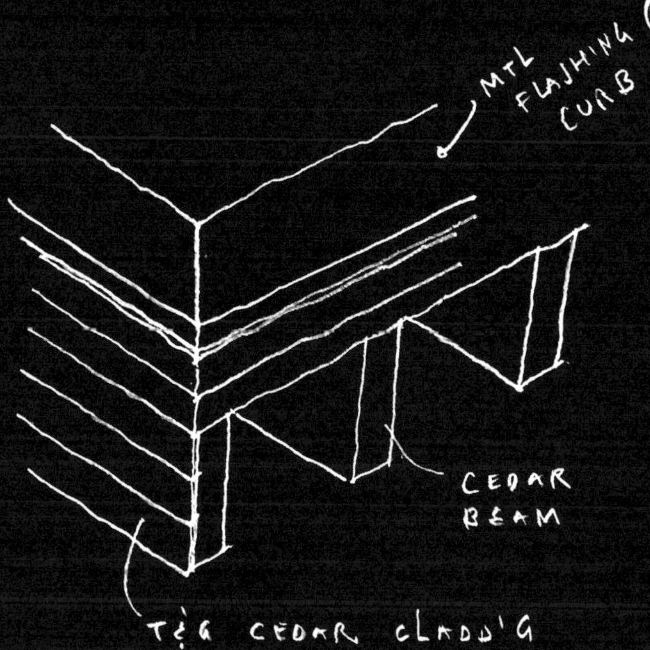
MTL
FLASHING @
CURB
CEDAR
BEAM
T&G CEDAR CLADD'G

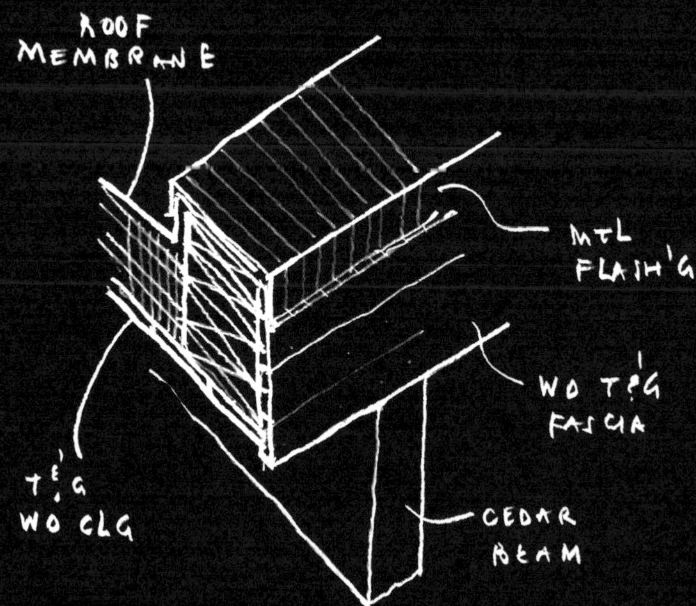
ROOF
MEMBRANE
MTL
FLASH'G
WD T&G
FASCIA
T&G
WD CLG
CEDAR
BEAM

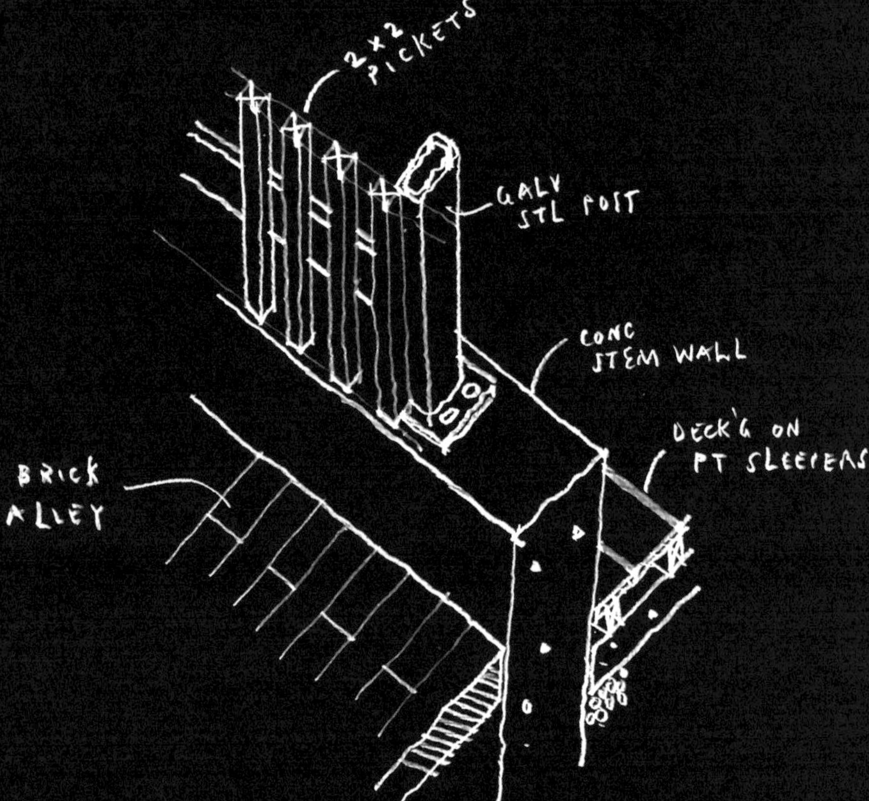
2×2
PICKETS
GALV
STL POST
CONC
STEM WALL
DECK'G ON
PT SLEEPERS
BRICK
ALLEY

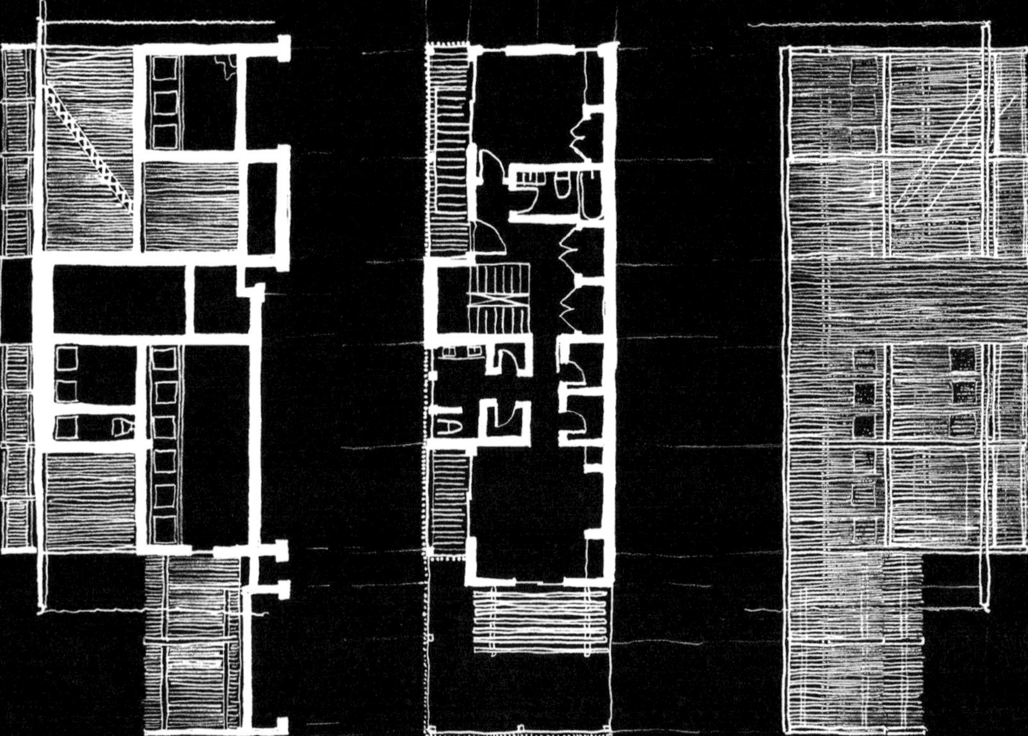

BROWN HOUSE

Overbeck Alley, Washington, DC

On an empty alley lot, gather:

1 precut BamCore kit
Equal parts BamCore kit to cellulose insulation and hempwool
1 truckbed black locust sticks (still green)
1 truckbed white oak sticks
1 truckbed cork flooring
2 front doors
3 sliding glass doors
14 double-pane awning windows and 4 casement windows
1 skylight, pitched to drain
Reclaimed bronze fixtures, handles, and pulls
1 cork kitchen countertop
1 pallet of plywood for kitchen cabinets
11 planters
2 truckbeds of soil
Copper flashing

---

1. Assemble, fill, and dress Bamcore kit with cork black locust, white oak, and copper.

2. Top with sloped membrane roof of any type, capped with corrugated metal planters.

3. Add skylights, windows, and doors.

4. Wrap house and property in white oak slatting.

5. Introduce copper flashing, gutters, and rain chains to taste.

6. Let sit.

LONG FENCE

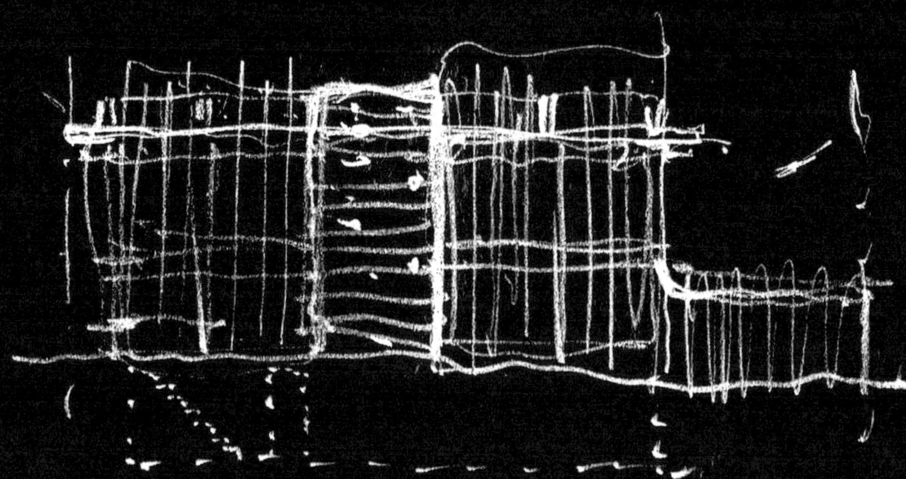

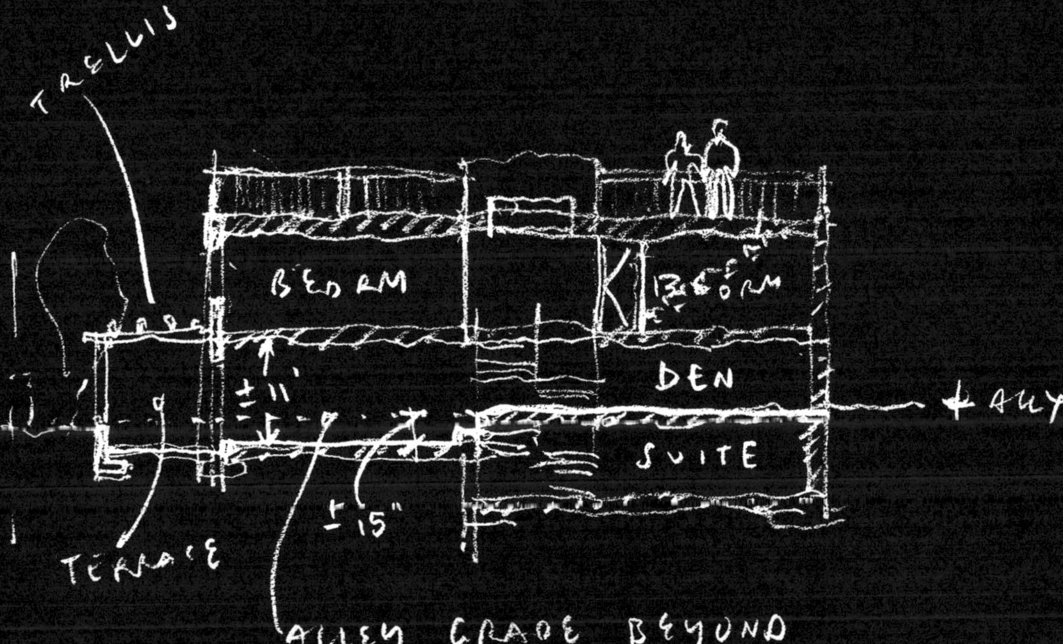
TRELLIS
BEDRM
DEN
ALLY
SUITE
±11"
±15"
TERRACE
ALLEY GRADE BEYOND

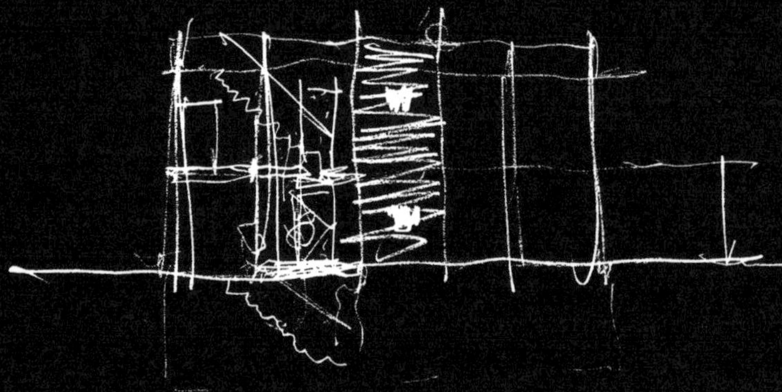

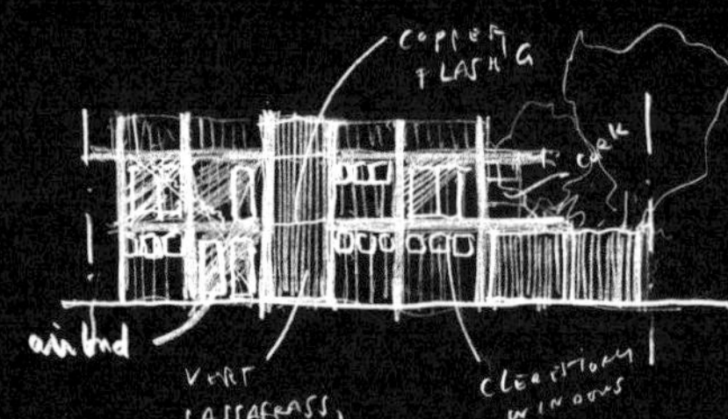
COPPER FLASHNG
OAK
VERT SASSAFRASS, SIM @ FENCE
CLERESTORY WINDOWS

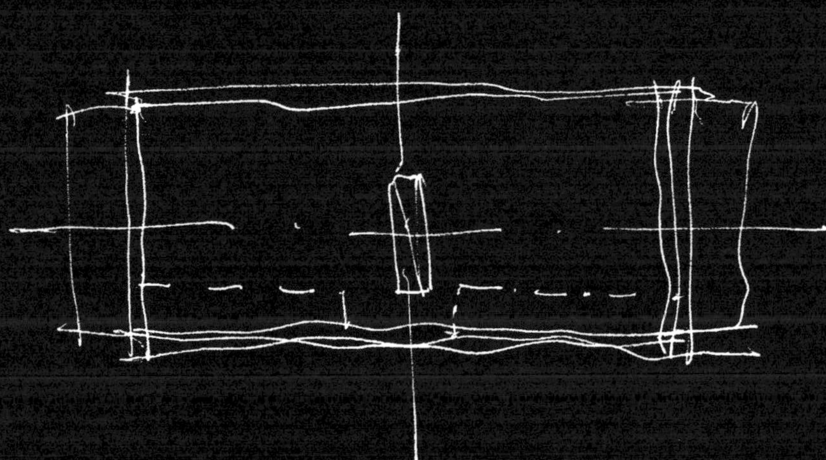

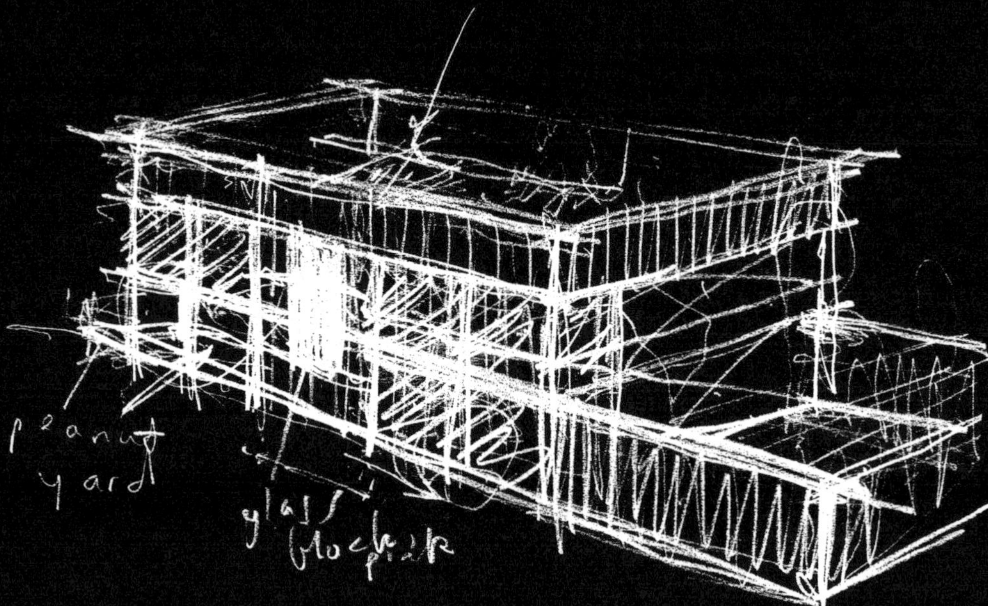
peanut yard
glass block pier

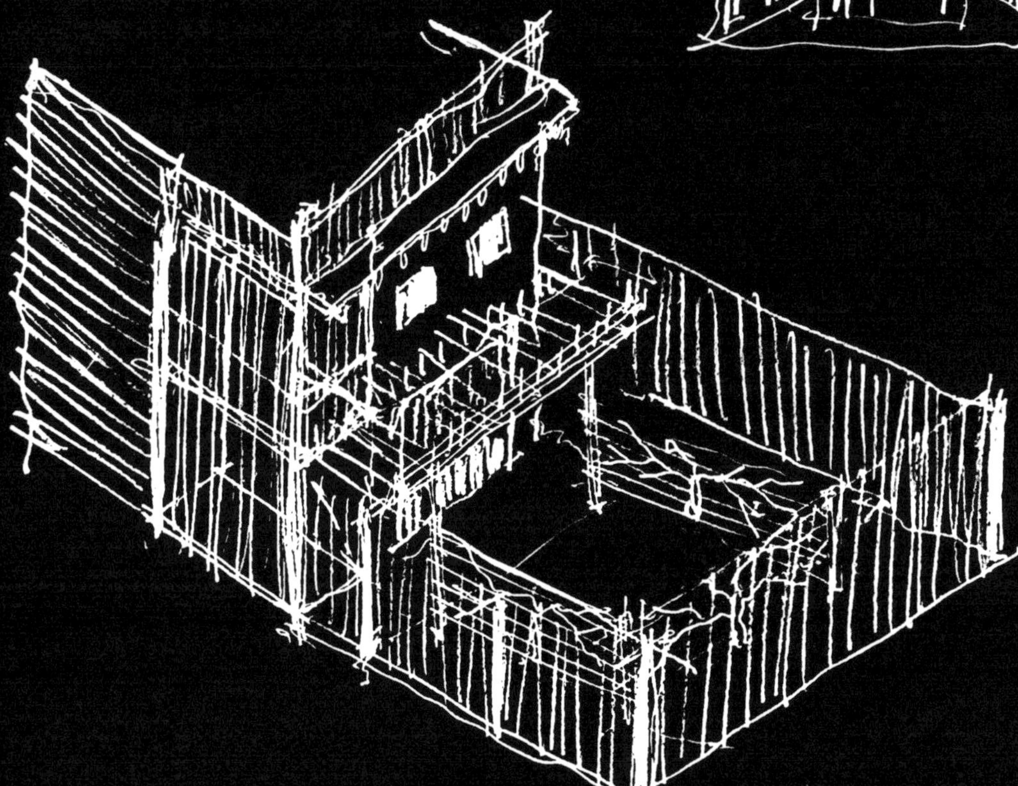

23 OVERBECK AL
PUSH

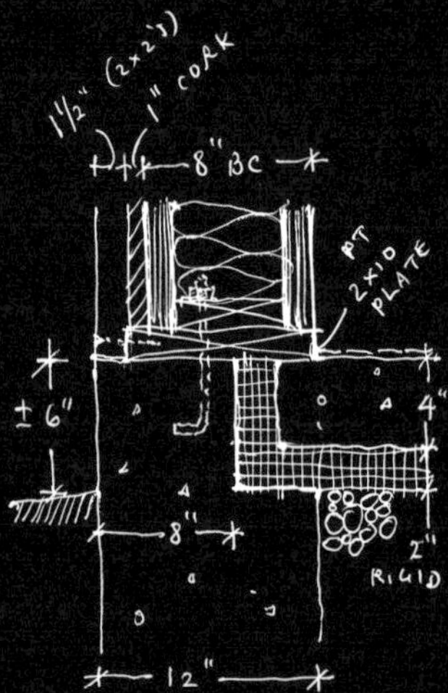
1 1/2" (2x2's)
1" CORK
8" BC
PT 2X10 PLATE
± 6"
4"
8"
2" RIGID
12"

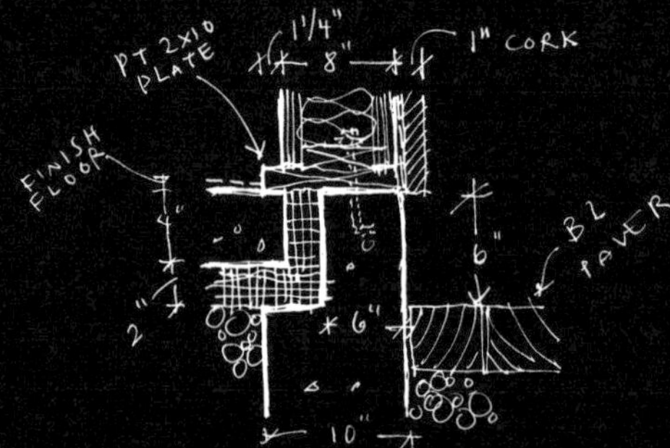
PT 2X10 PLATE
1 1/4"
8"
1" CORK
FINISH FLOOR
6"
BL PAVER
2"
6"
10"

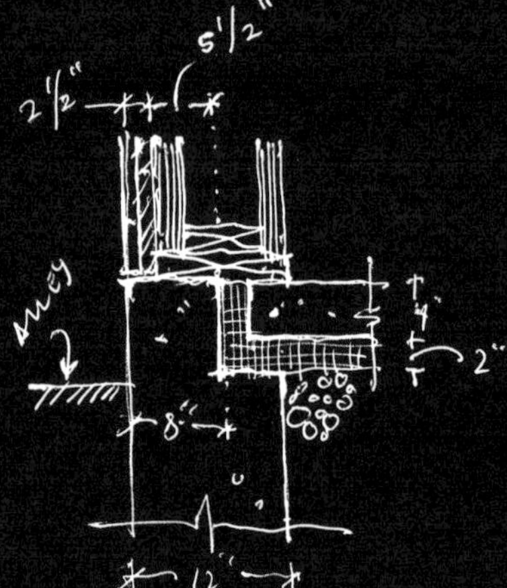
5 1/2"
2 1/2"
ALLEY
4"
2"
8"
12"

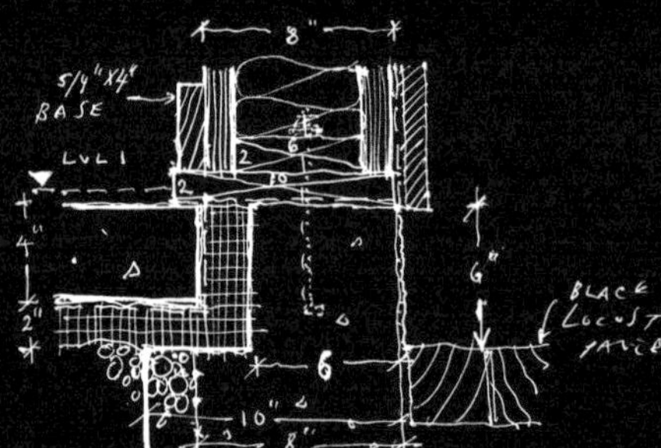
8"
5/4" X 4" BASE
LVL 1
4"
2"
6"
BLACK LOCUST PAVER
6
10"
8"

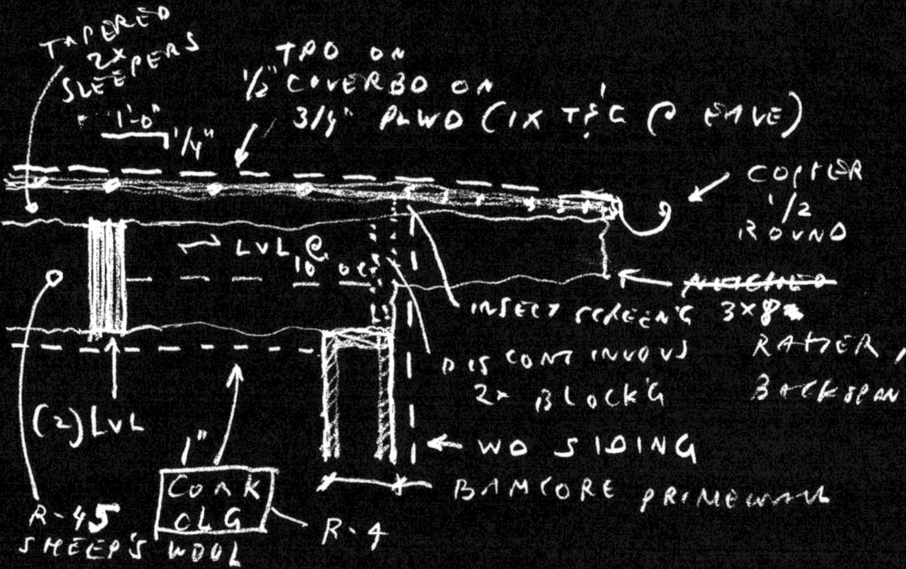
TAPERED 2x SLEEPERS
1'-0"
1/4"
TPO ON 1/2" COVERBD ON 3/4" PLWD (1X T&G @ EAVE)
COPPER 1/2 ROUND
LVL @ 16" OC
NOTCHED
INSECT SCREEN'G
3x8 RAFTER, BACKSPAN
DISCONTINUOUS 2x BLOCK'G
(2) LVL
1"
WD SIDING
CORK CLG
BAMCORE PRIMEWALL
R-45 SHEEP'S WOOL
R-4

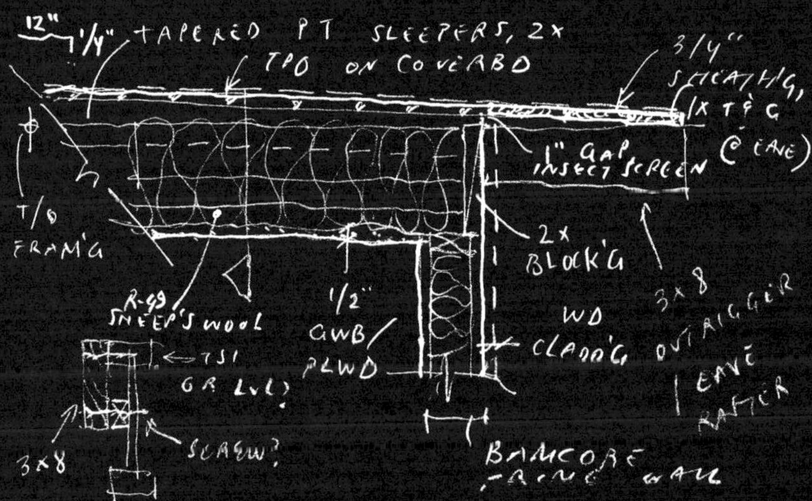
12"
1 1/4"
TAPERED PT SLEEPERS, 2X
TPO ON COVERBD
3/4" SHEATH'G, 1X T&G (@ EAVE)
1" GAP INSECT SCREEN
T/O FRAM'G
2X BLOCK'G
3x8 OUTRIGGER
R-49 SHEEP'S WOOL
1/2" GWB/ PLWD
WD CLADD'G
EAVE RAFTER
TJI OR LVL?
3x8
SCREW?
BAMCORE FRAME WALL

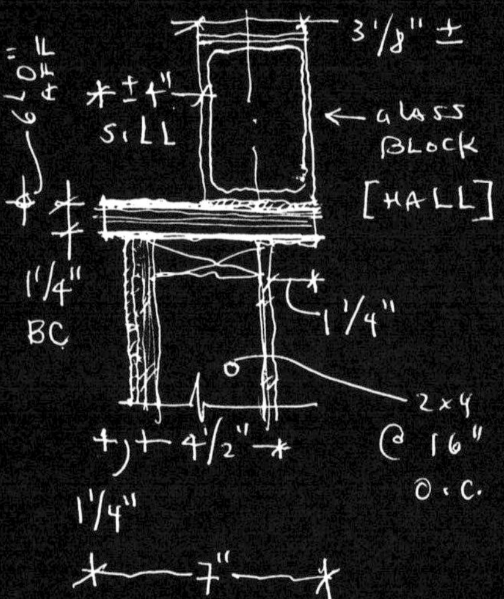
3 1/8" ±
6'0" FF
± 4" SILL
← GLASS BLOCK
[HALL]
1 1/4" BC
1 1/4"
2×4 @ 16" O.C.
4 1/2"
1 1/4"
7"

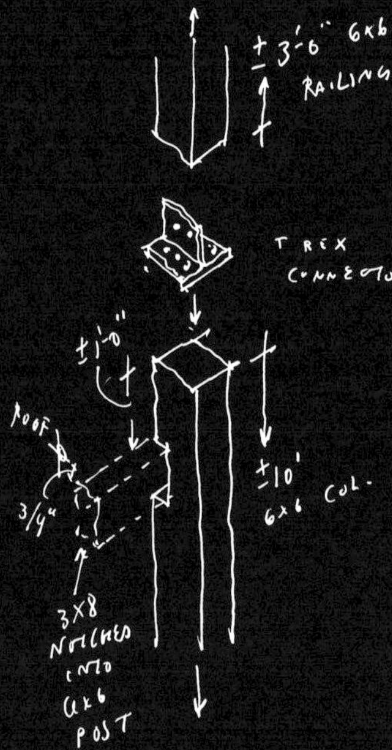
± 3'-6" 6x6 RAILING
TREX CONNECTOR
± 1'-0"
ROOF
3/4"
3×8 NOTCHED INTO 6x6 POST
± 10' 6x6 COL.

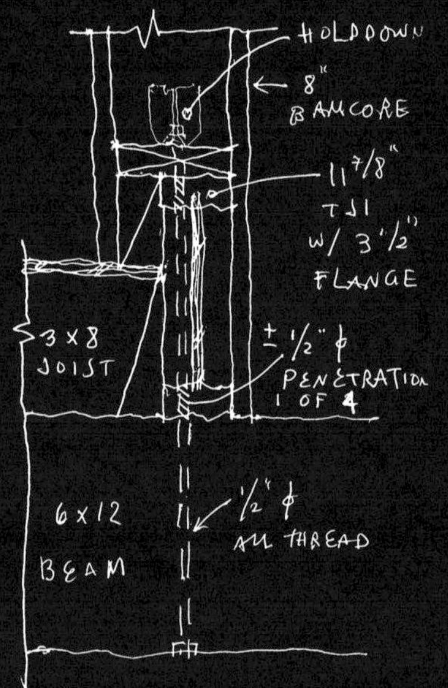
HOLDDOWN
← 8" BAMCORE
11 7/8" TJI W/ 3 1/2" FLANGE
3×8 JOIST
± 1/2" ϕ PENETRATION 1 OF 4
6×12 BEAM
1/2" ϕ ALL THREAD

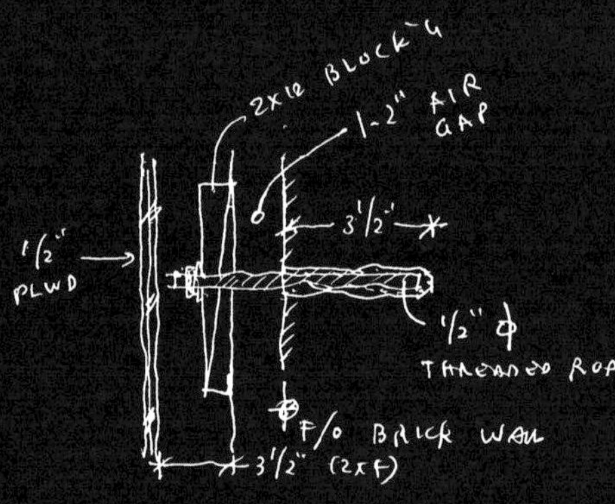
2x12 BLOCK'G
1-2" AIR GAP
3 1/2"
1/2" PLWD →
1/2" ϕ THREADED ROD
F/O BRICK WALL
3 1/2" (2×F)

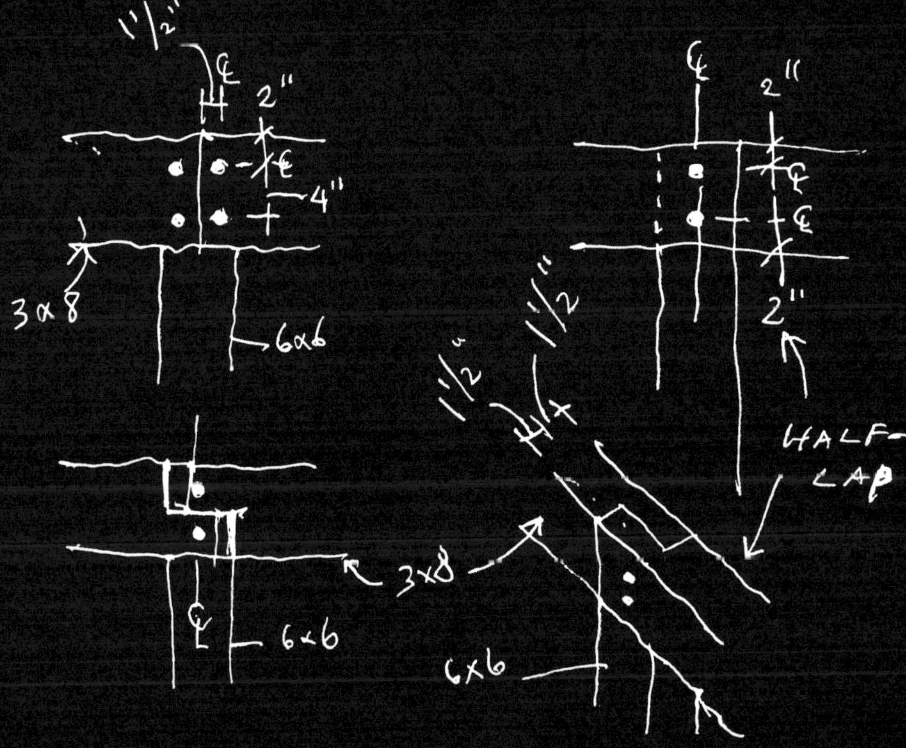
1 1/2"
℄
2"
℄
4"
3x8
6x6
℄
2"
℄
℄
2"
1 1/2"
1 1/2"
HALF-
LAP
3x8
℄
6x6
6x6

EAST

BOSCH
BOSCH

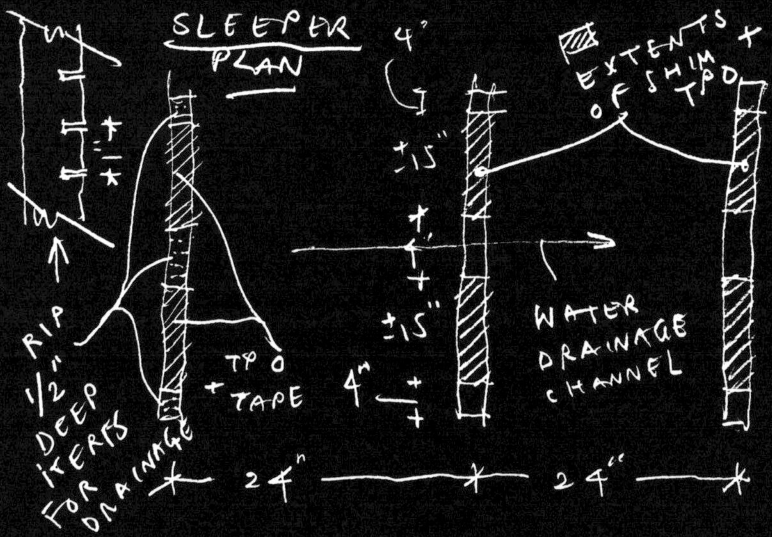

SLEEPER PLAN
4"
±15"
±15"
4"
EXTENTS OF SHIM + TPO
WATER DRAINAGE CHANNEL
TPO + TAPE
RIP 1/2" DEEP KERFS FOR DRAINAGE
24"
24"

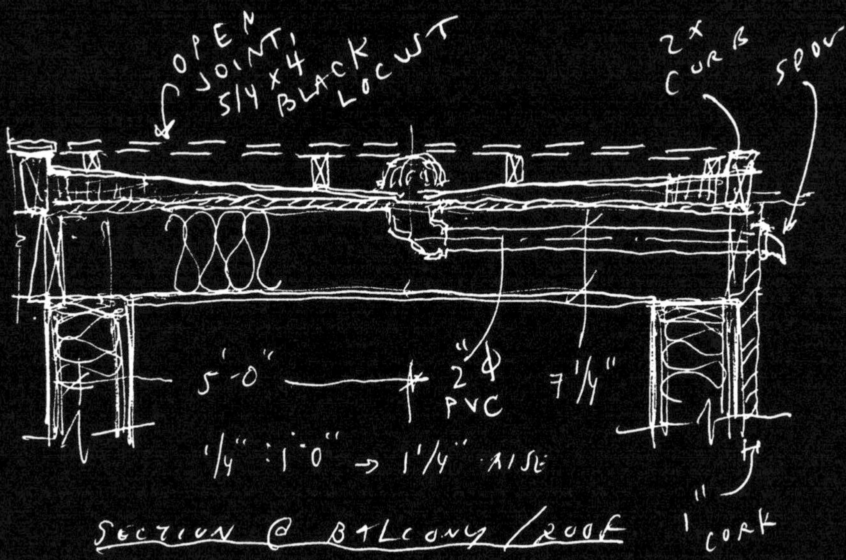

OPEN JOINT, 5/4 x 4 BLACK LOCUST
2x CURB
SPOU
5'-0"
2" Φ PVC
7 1/4"
1/4" : 1'-0" → 1 1/4" RISE
1" CORK
SECTION @ BALCONY / ROOF

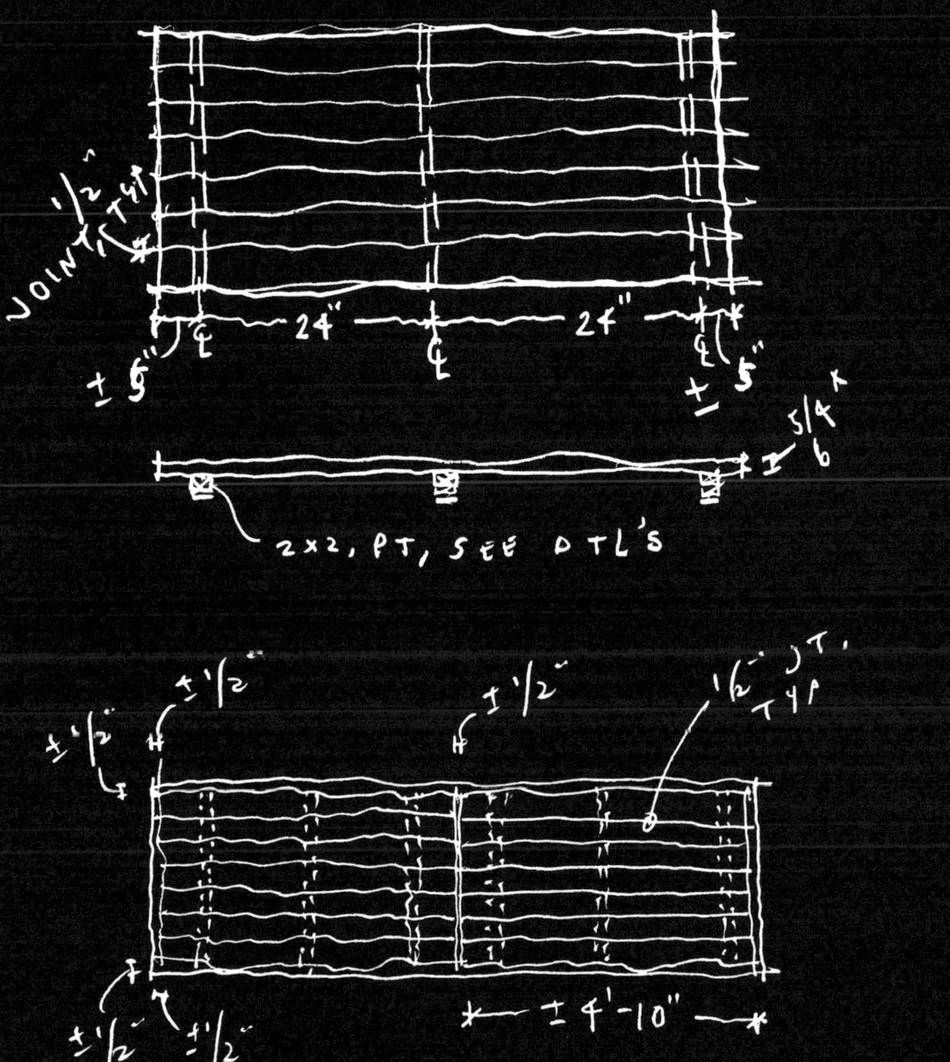

BALCONY DECK PLAN

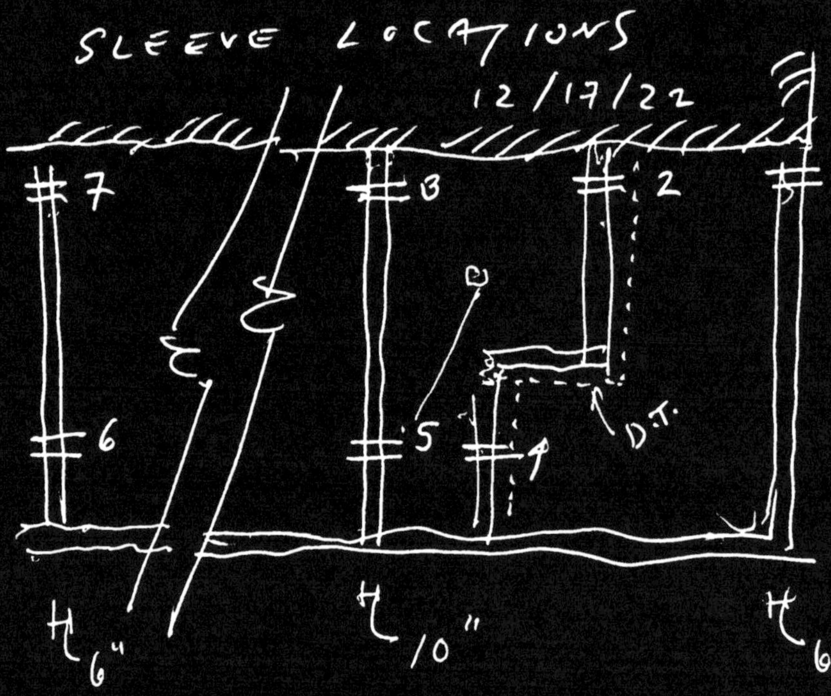
SLEEVE LOCATIONS
12/17/22
7
8
2
6
5
4
D.T.
6"
10"
6"

To Heal the Earth
OVERGROWN
ARMITAGE'S NATIVE PLANTS
GARDEN REVOLUTION
DARKE & TALLAMY
THE LIVING LANDSCAPE
PLANTS

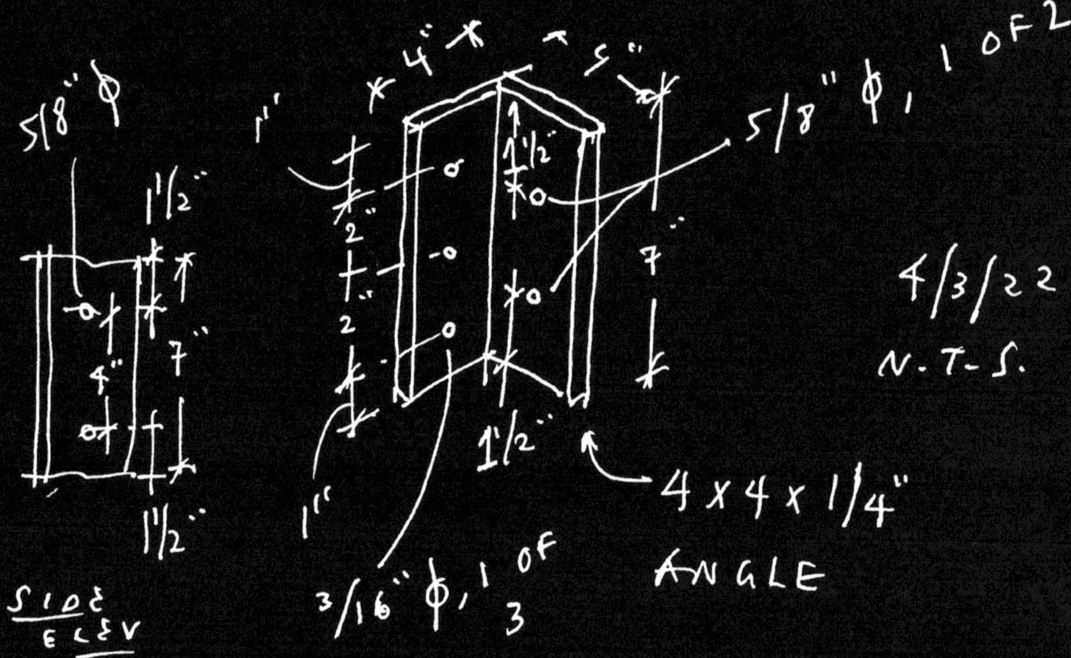
5/8" ϕ
1½"
7"
4"
1½"
SIDE ELEV
1"
4"
5"
5/8" ϕ, 1 OF 2
1½"
2
2
7"
1"
1½"
4 x 4 x 1/4"
ANGLE
3/16" ϕ, 1 OF 3
4/3/22
N.T.S.

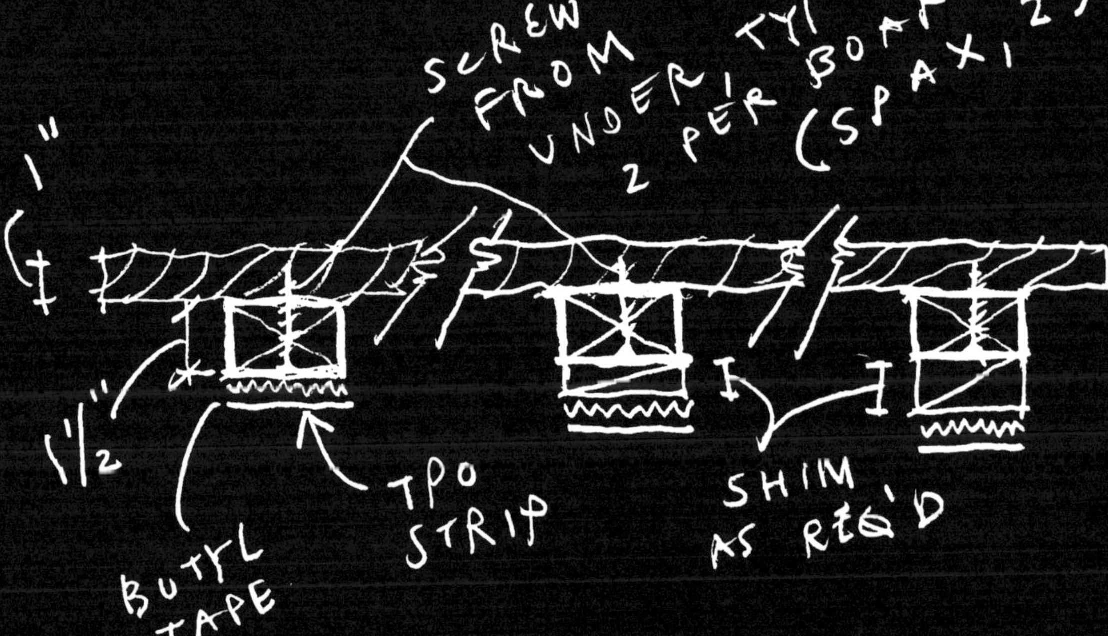
SCREW FROM UNDER, TYP 2 PER BOARD (SPAX, 2")
1"
1 1/2"
BUTYL TAPE
TPO STRIP
SHIM AS REQ'D

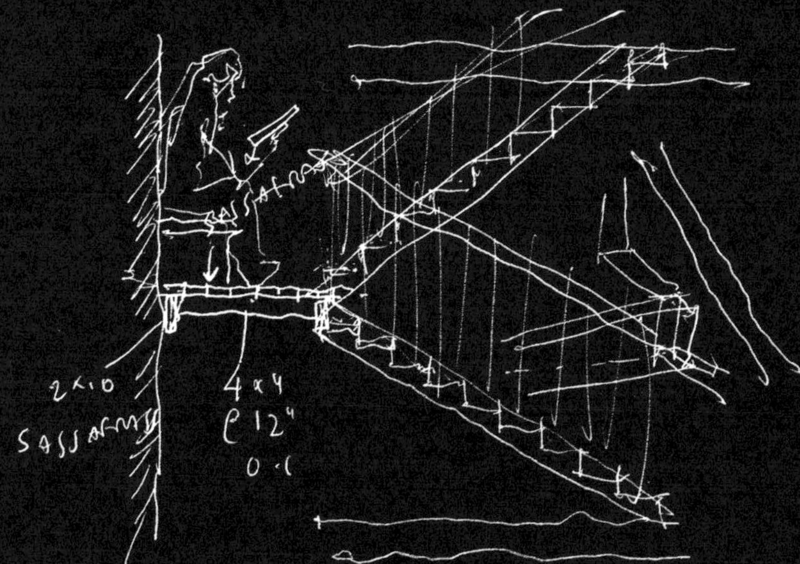
2x10
SASSAFRAS
4x4
@ 12"
O.C

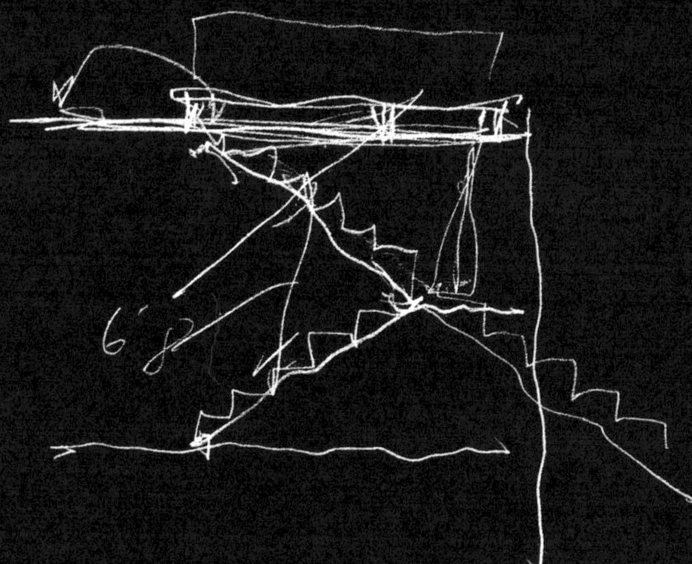
6'8"

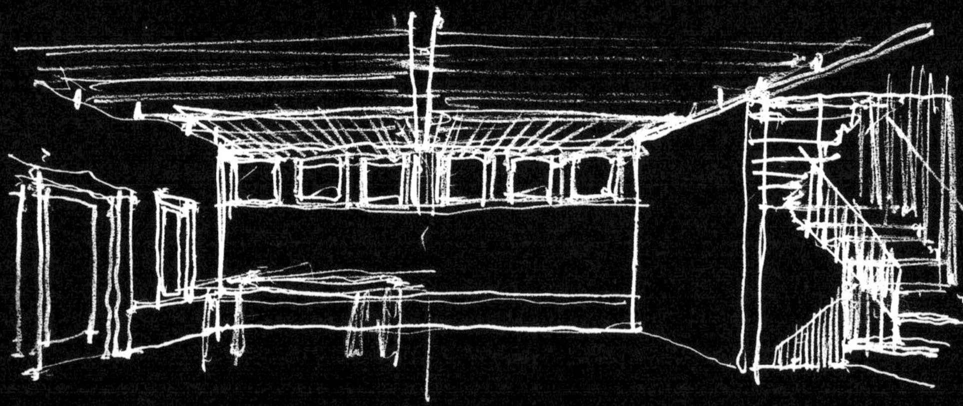

LONG FENCE

HOUSE CUISINE

As the settlement of Earth becomes increasingly dense with unhealthy buildings, people are becoming aware of the biological intimacy between buildings and humans. Inhabiting a building necessarily means inhaling it at a molecular level— in this sense we consume our buildings.

In the Mid-Atlantic region, a way to mitigate the impacts of a home on your health and instead promote good health is to build a tightly sealed, well-ventilated, and densely insulated shell made from natural woods and grasses with little mechanical or chemical processing. The ideal BLDUS material palette of ingredients is, unsurprisingly, similar to materials found in indigenous construction in the region: wood, bark, willow, bamboo, wool, and stone. However expansive, the material assemblies in BLDUS projects represent a small fraction of the natural material abundance available today.

The following photographs are not quite recipes, but are instead more like sketches for future recipes, each offering itself as the seed of an architectural palette. Materials with obvious identities mix with more obscure components. There are no BLDUS nutritional facts for a material's health—we trust our palate and our gut to define our taste.

MATERIALS

Page 204 Trace paper, BamCore whitewashed with Real Milk Paint, BamCore painted white with Real Milk Paint, cork flooring, Accoya wood siding, birch plywood, bamboo rhyzome.

205 Walnut cutting board, Barkhouse tulip poplar bark siding, Buckingham slate threshold segment.

206 Cork flooring, hemp rope, Havelock sheeps wool insulation.

207 Cork wall covering, wood fence post from John Egn er's farm in Andes, NY, split BamCore Gen2, bamboo coaster.

208 Resawn Timber Co Atlantic white cedar select tight knot burnt brushed & selaed, Resawn Timber Co Monogatari Cypress #2 common burnt brushed & sealed, Barkhouse tulip poplar bark.

209 Wood fence post from John Egner's farm in Andes, NY, cork wall covering.

210 Wood dish, Amorim expanded cork siding, charred BamCore Gen1 panel, BamCore Gen1 panel, Cupaclad slate, Resawn Timber Co charred kebony siding.

211 Purple slate, Resawn Timber Co Nero thermally modified radiata pine cladding, cherry wood.

212–213 Century-old wood beam from Anacostia house charred during fire.

214 Reed bowl, Resawn Timber Co charred cedar siding, green slate, Resawn Timber Co Tatami white oak glulam, bamboo charcoal.

215 Century-old wood beam from Anacostia house charred during house fire.

216 Copper dish, cork wall covering, Buckingham slate, bamboo charcoal.

217 Aluminum Reinke shake, pine, BamCore Gen3, black locust.

218 Accoya wood roof shake, black locust wood, strawboard, sake cups.

219 Photo foil, copper dish, colored concrete samples (Savannah Ivory, White, Blush, Lite Beige, Clay Pink, Red, Crimson Red, Georgia Red, Canyon Brown, Dark Brown, Charcoal, Black).

220 Buckingham slate, bamboo and wood sticks, white zip ties.

221 Purple slate, bamboo and wood coaster, mud dauber nest.

222 Bird nest.

223 Door section by Fabio Designs on wood sticks.

224 Hemp cord.

225 Colored concrete samples (Santan, Lite Beige, Canyon Brown, Red, Wine, Charcoal, Black) with blue tape in bamboo basket.

226 Hemp insulation, Maibec cedar siding, Amorim cork siding, cherry wood.

227 Weavecore bamboo plywood, bamboo cup, wood and bamboo sticks, black zip ties.

228 Purple slate, Resawn Timber Co #2 common burnt brushed and sealed Monogatari cypress, copper placemat, wood stump.

HOUSE CUISINE

229 Rattan basket, BarkHouse tulip poplar bark, model of US Capitol dome.

230 Resawn Timber Co #2 common burnt brushed and sealed Monogatari cypress, cork wall covering, BarkHouse tulip poplar bark cladding, copper roofing nails.

231 Trace paper, black locust stick, copper wire.

232 Charred cypress and poplar wood, copper wire.

233 BamCore Gen1, wood and bamboo coaster, wasp nest.

234 Driftwood, mica.

235 Resawn Timber Co charred cedar siding, Accoya cedar roof shingle, chalk.

236 Resawn Timber Co #2 common burnt brushed & sealed Monogatari cypress, aluminum Reinke shake, Suberra ultra high density cork, wood biscuits, twist-on wire connectors.

237 Reed basket, BarkHouse birch bark interior wall covering, bamboo skewers.

238 Mulberry wood, aluminum and copper cut tacks.

239 Resawn Timber Co Manuka thermally modified radiata pine cladding, cork bark peeled off a knot, copper wire, orange flagging tape.

240 BamCore Gen3 with sample stains, Omni Block insulated concrete block without insulation.

241 Resawn Timber Co Amity European white oak flooring, brass wire, Resawn Timber Co Kinoko reclaimed hemlock interior cladding.

242 Paper wasp nest, oak wood.

243 CaliBamboo Rustic Beachwood fossilized wide solid strand bamboo flooring, Resawn Timber Co Kinoko reclaimed hemlock cladding, WeCork Ivory cork flooring, aluminum & copper cut tacks, oak flat head plugs, cable clips.

244 Plywood, cork wall claddings, oak wood.

245 Cork wall claddings, foam sill seal.

246 Purple and green slate, historic pine cladding, Amorim expanded cork cladding.

247 Models of Poplar Forest, Monticello, and Lady Freedom on strawboard.

248 Bamboo cutting board, BamCore Gen2, BamCore Gen3, mica, Buckingham slate, Tennessee pink marble, bamboo strips.

249 Bird nest in sake cup on BamCore Gen2.

250 Wood basket, BamCore Gen3, bamboo and wood sticks.

251 Cherry wood, Resawn Timber Co Vette charred Kebony, model of the House of Seven Gables.

252 Copper dish, bamboo and wood sticks, PlybooStrand dimensional lumber.

253 Richlite, dirt.

254 BamCore Gen2, bamboo stick, bamboo coaster.

255 BamCore Gen1, wood and bamboo coaster, mud dauber nest.

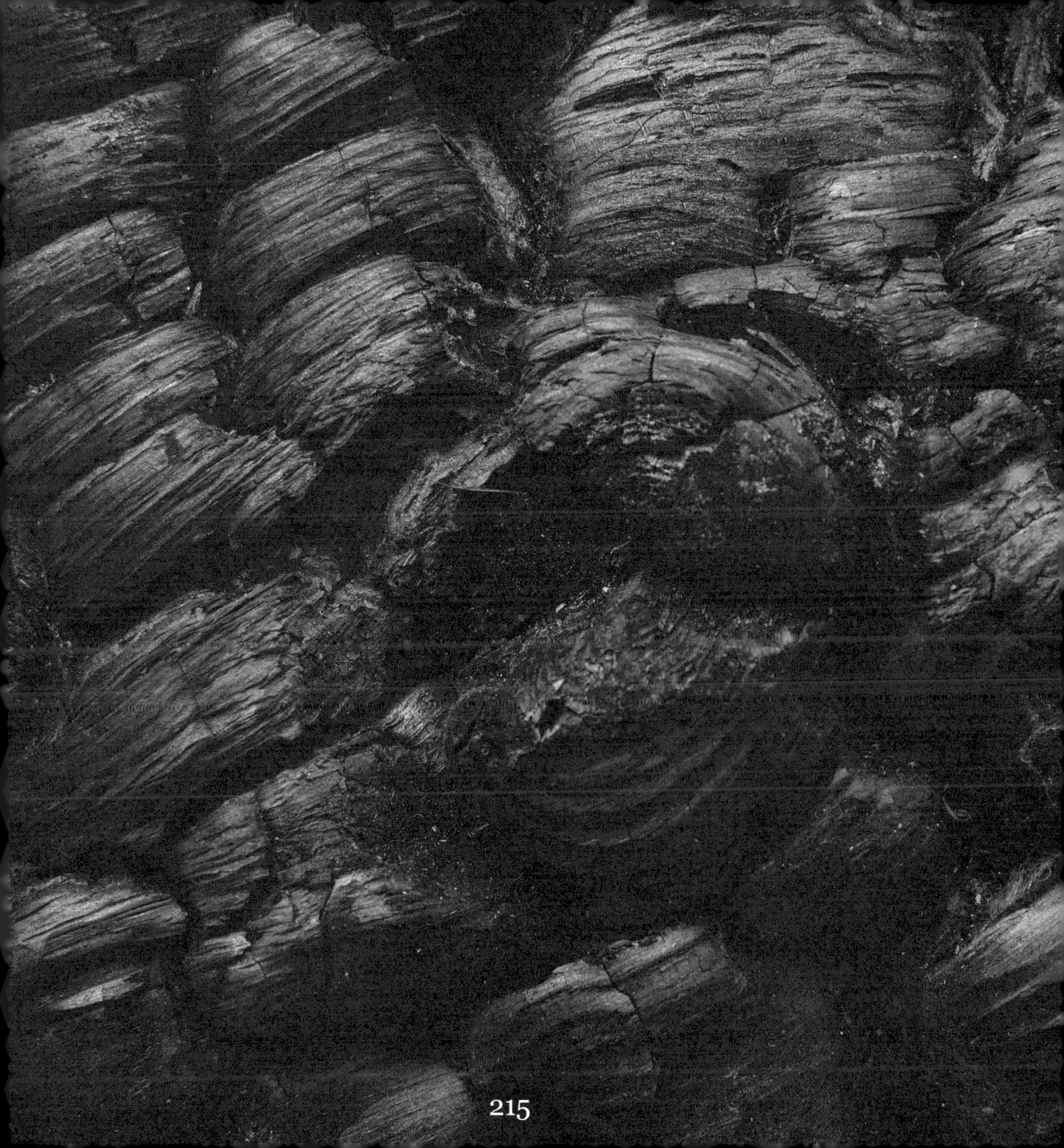

BACK OF HOUSE

The following houses were designed for situations in and around DC. They were not built for a variety of reasons, instead living on–in the hearts and minds of the clients that first dreamed them into existence and in the BLDUS design ecology–in pristine condition, spared the harsh realities of construction, occupation, weathering, and maintenance. Models allow ideas to take form as physical entities despite their failure to materialize into tangible shelter.

These models are synesthetic expressions of space, taste, light and sound: details implied with expressive connections, bits of food incorporated to elicit multi-sensory responses, landscapes sculpted with common pantry items, garnishes adding the suggestion of tactility. Rather than being relegated to the archives, these unbuilt designs are in some ways more vital than built projects. The fabrication of fantasy allows for the development of these delicious moments, still unrestricted by reality. Therein lies a secret of the sauce, critical to the BLDUS back-of-house.

The back-of-house is not only where our ideas take shape, but where most of these designs are rooted: in the neighborhoods surrounding the US Capitol, in the shadows of the People's House. This community of DC residents works to support national and international governance, unrecognized by most fellow Americans yet essential for the success of the world. The nation's back-of-house workers, situated behind The House.

Back-of-house homes for back-of-House neighborhoods.

LONG HOUSE

Piney Branch, Washington, DC

On an oddly shaped lot with high visibility from the street
but limited exposure from neighbors, combine:

1 precut BamCore kit
Equal parts BamCore kit to wool insulation
Cedar beams and sticks
1 part cork : 1 part charred cedar boards : 1 part cedar shingles
A few rolls of insect screening
Some cork flooring
Some skylights
Some exterior glass doors
Some sliding glass doors
Some awning windows

---

1. Construct and stuff the BamCore panels.

2. Top with cedar shingles and copper gutters. Array solar panels.

3. Dress BamCore kit, alternating between layers of cork and cedar layers and sprinkling copper roofing nails throughout.

4. Sprinkle in windows, doors, skylights, and stairs.

5. Frame the screened porch, entry porch, and exterior stairs. Then tautly wrap the screened porch in insect screening.

6. Finish interior to taste.

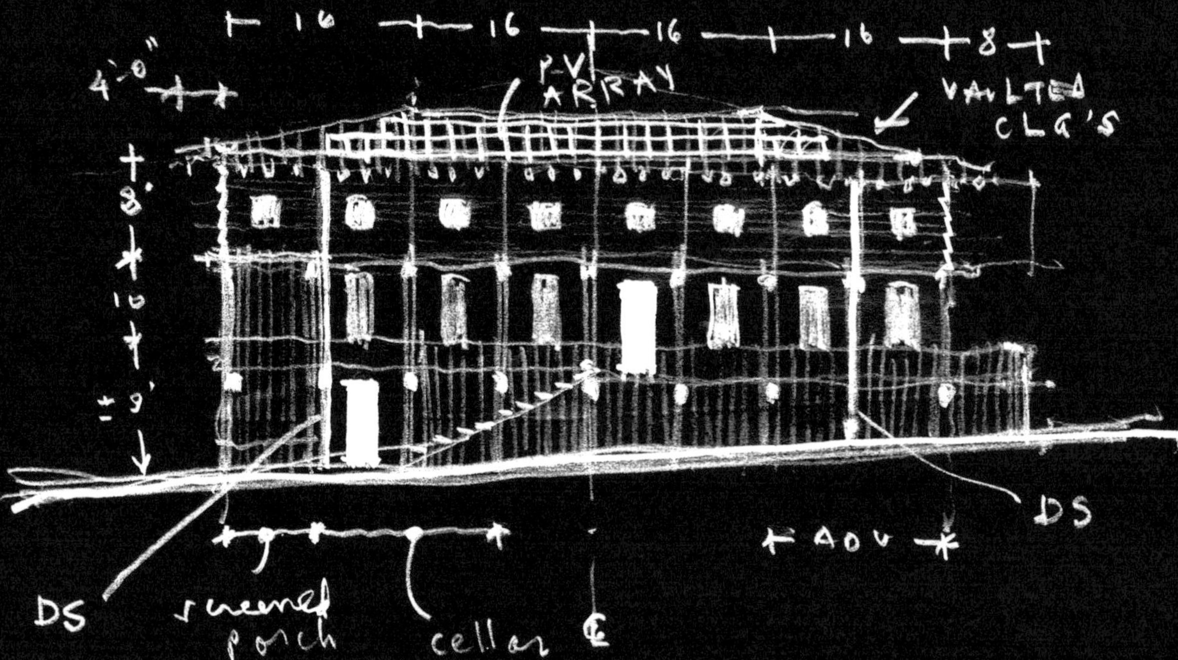
16
16
16
16
8
4'-0"
P-V ARRAY
VAULTED CLG'S
8'
10'
9'
DS
screened porch
cellar
DS
ADU

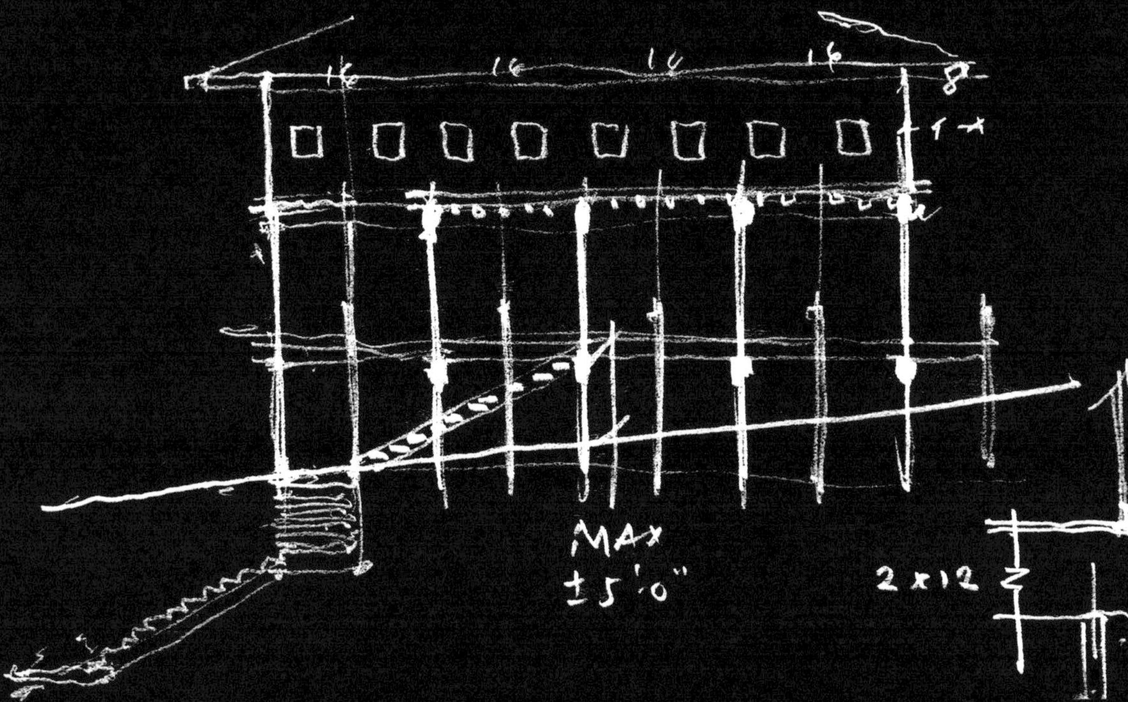
16
16
14
16
8
MAX
±5'0"
2 x 12

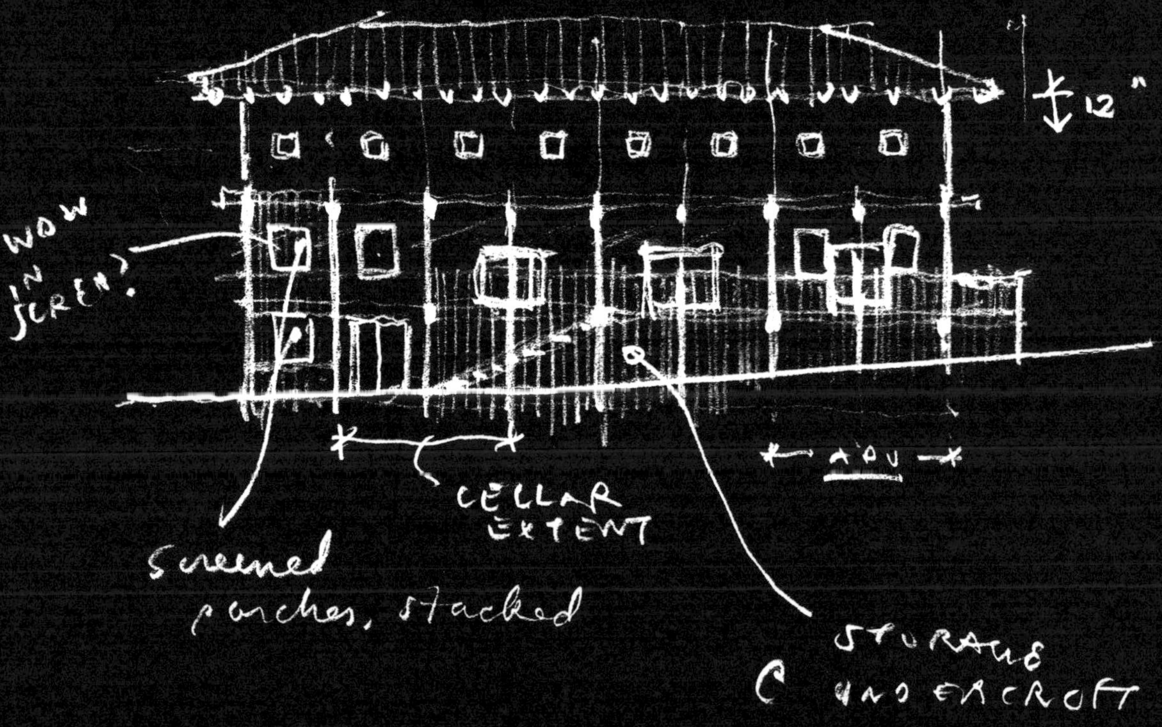
12"
WOW IN SCREEN!
ADU
CELLAR EXTENT
screened porches, stacked
STORAGE @ UNDERCROFT

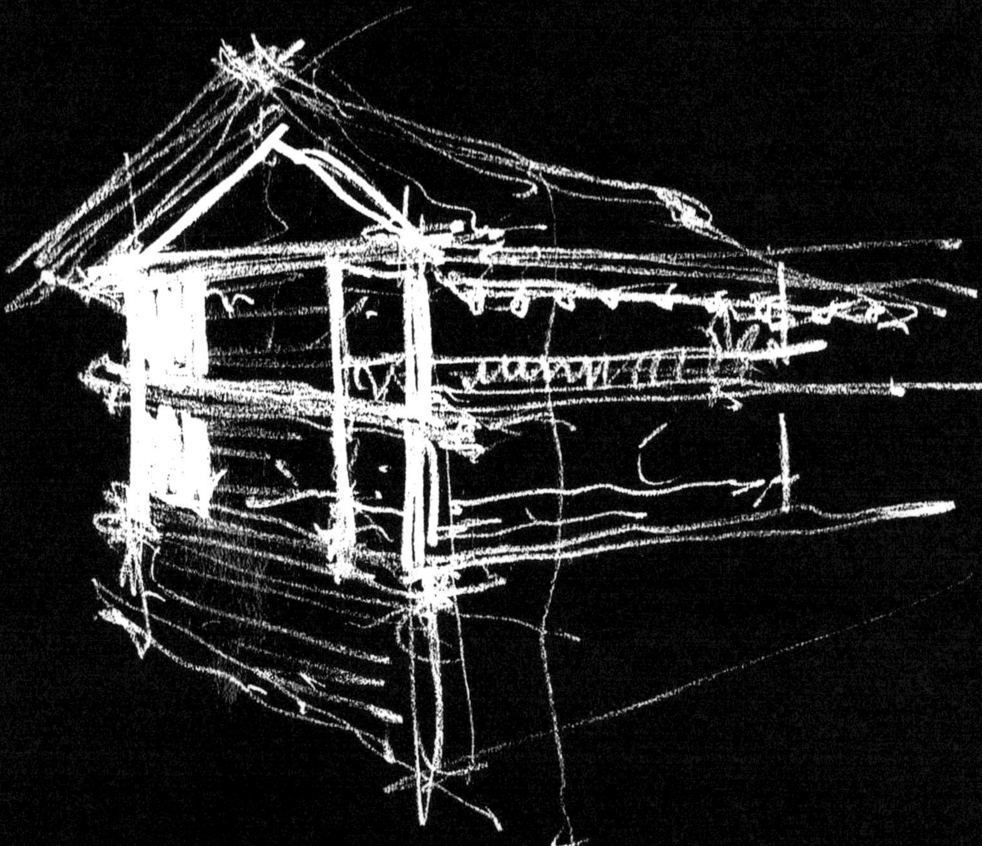

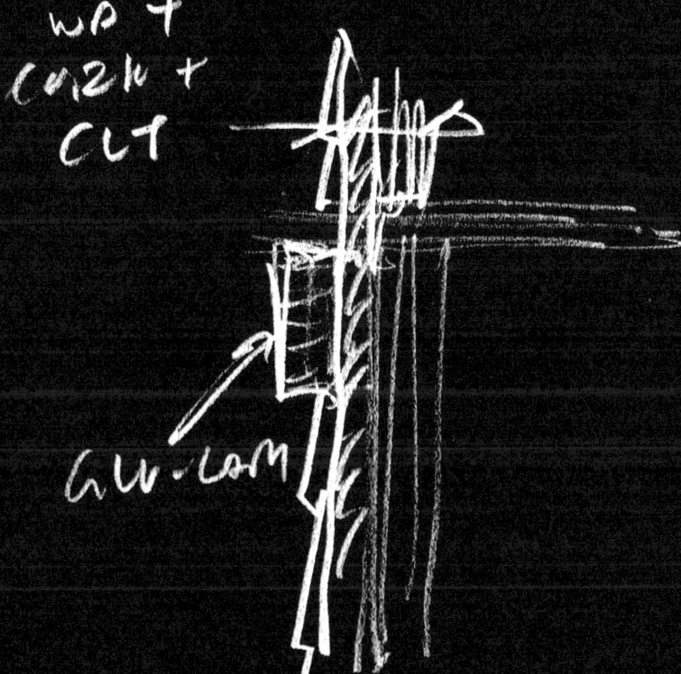
CLT

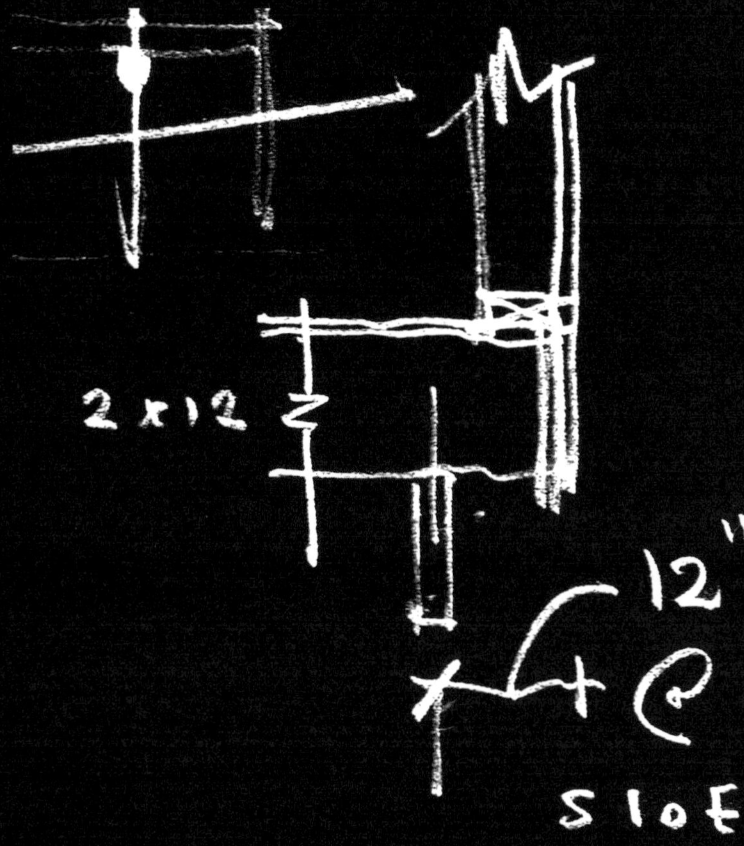

2x12
12"
S10E

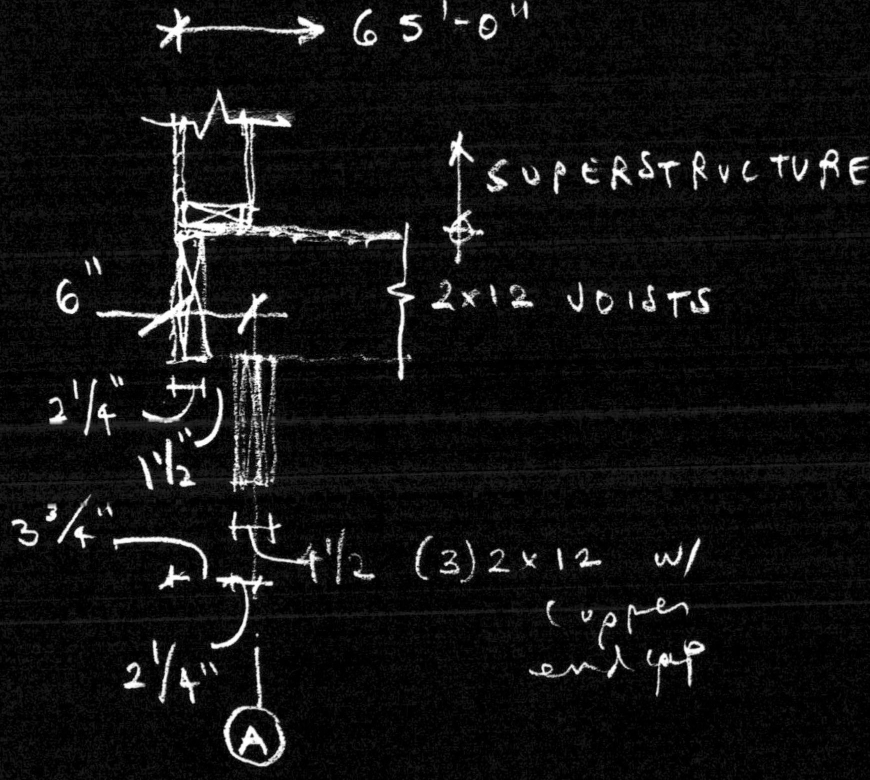

65'-0"
SUPERSTRUCTURE
6"
2x12 JOISTS
2 1/4"
1 1/2"
3 3/4"
1 1/2 (3) 2x12 w/
copper
end cap
2 1/4"
A

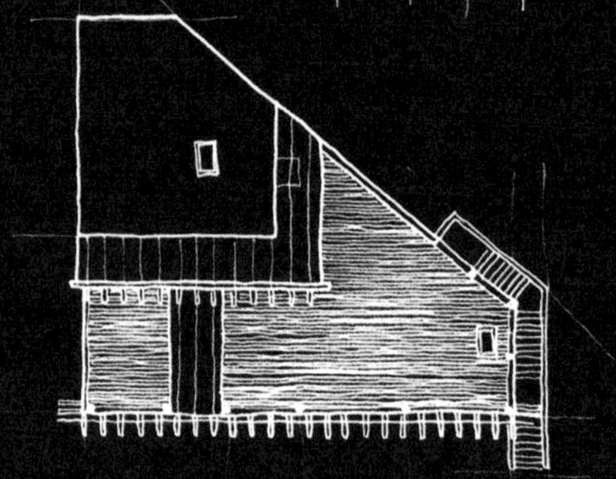

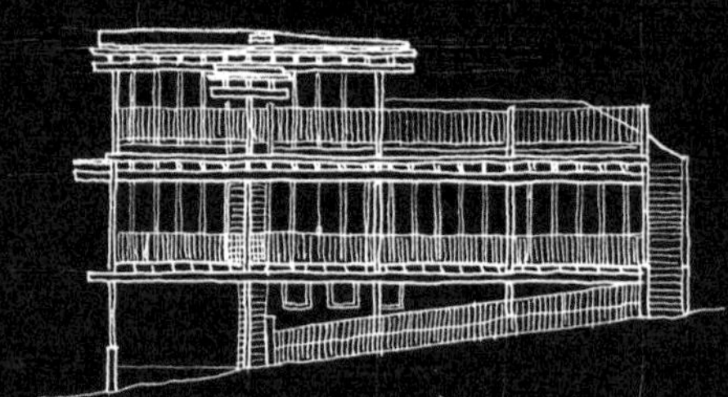

RAMBLE HOUSE

Penn Branch, Washington, DC

On a strange steeply sloped wedge-shaped scrap of land, tucked away in rolling hills, combine:

1 heavily reinforced retaining wall
A few truckloads of 2x12 joists
A dozen 6x6 glulam posts and just as many 4x12 glulam beams
Some cedar beams and sticks
Some cork siding
Some cork flooring
Some black locust roof decking
Some guardrail steel netting
Some skylights, exterior glass doors, and awning windows
A length of storefront windows
Brass fixtures, handles, and pulls
1 long copper gutter with two rain chains

---

1. Stabilize the slope; swirl in a retaining wall and foundation. Use the soil at another project.

2. Frame the walls, floors, and roofs; top with black locust decking.

3. Add windows, doors, skylights, stairs, then lift up a storefront window system along the broad side of the house.

4. Spread cork over side walls.

5. Wrap a metal mesh guardrail around the roof and veranda's locust stanchions.

6. Transfer kitchen and baths into the house.

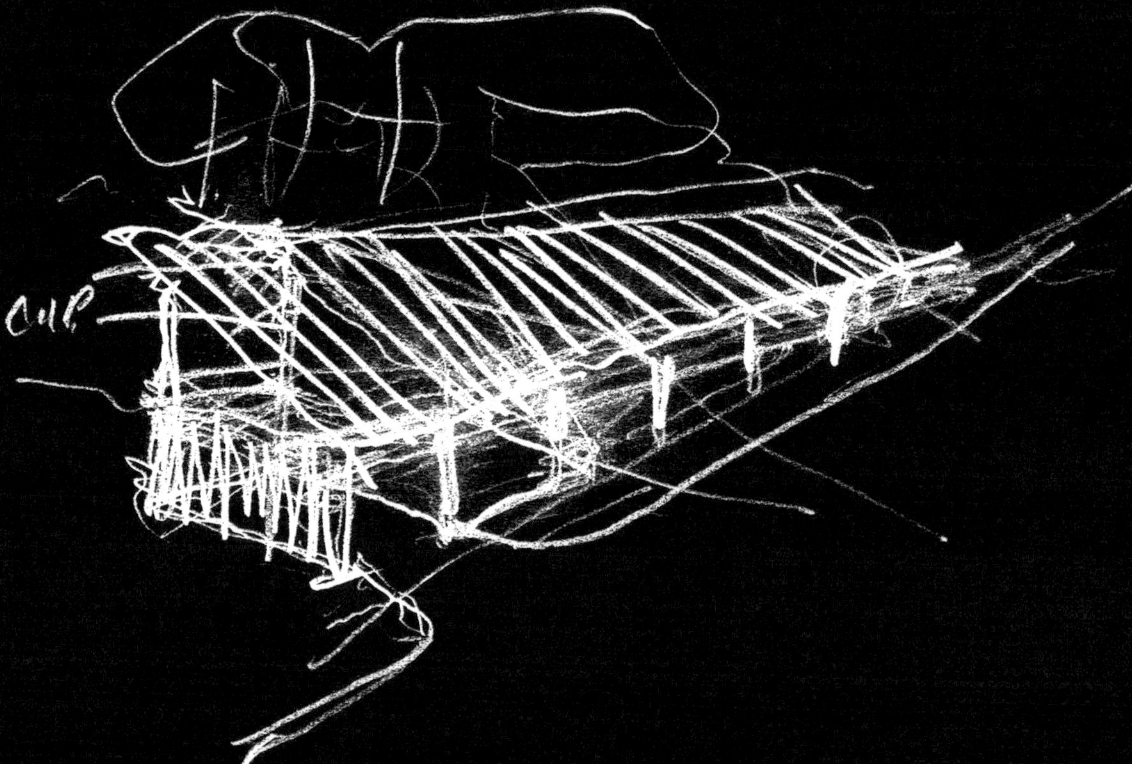
C.M.P.

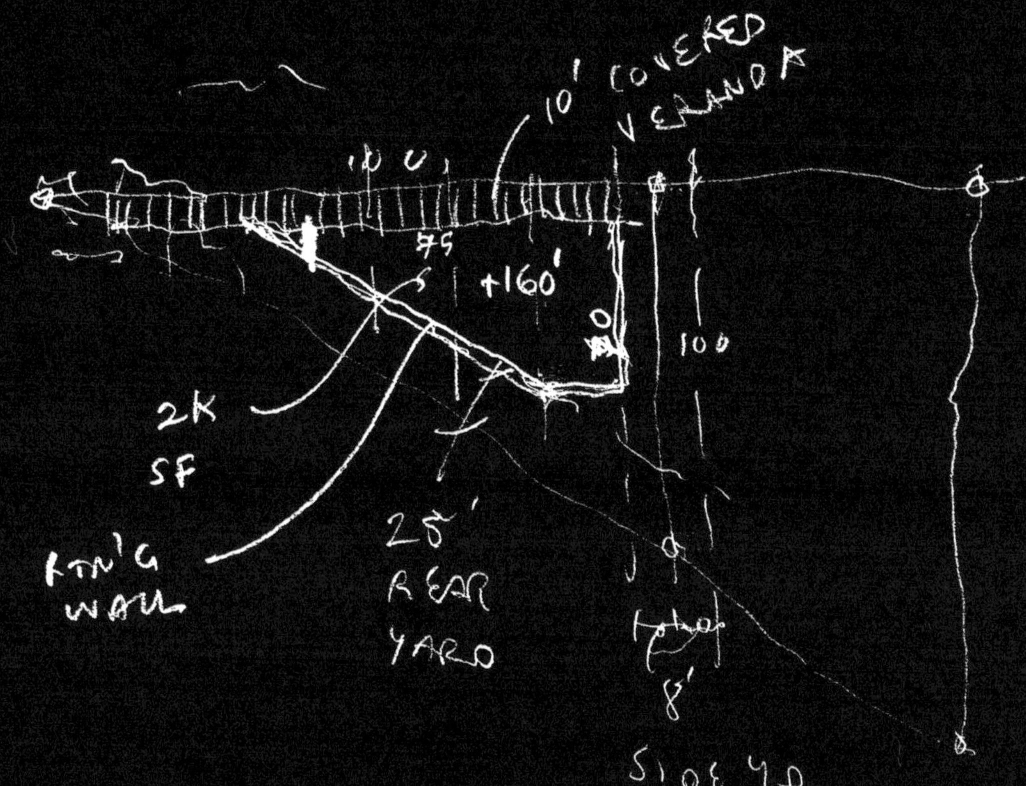
10' COVERED
VERANDA
100
75
+160'
100
2K
SF
RTN'G
WALL
28'
REAR
YARD
8'
SIDE YD

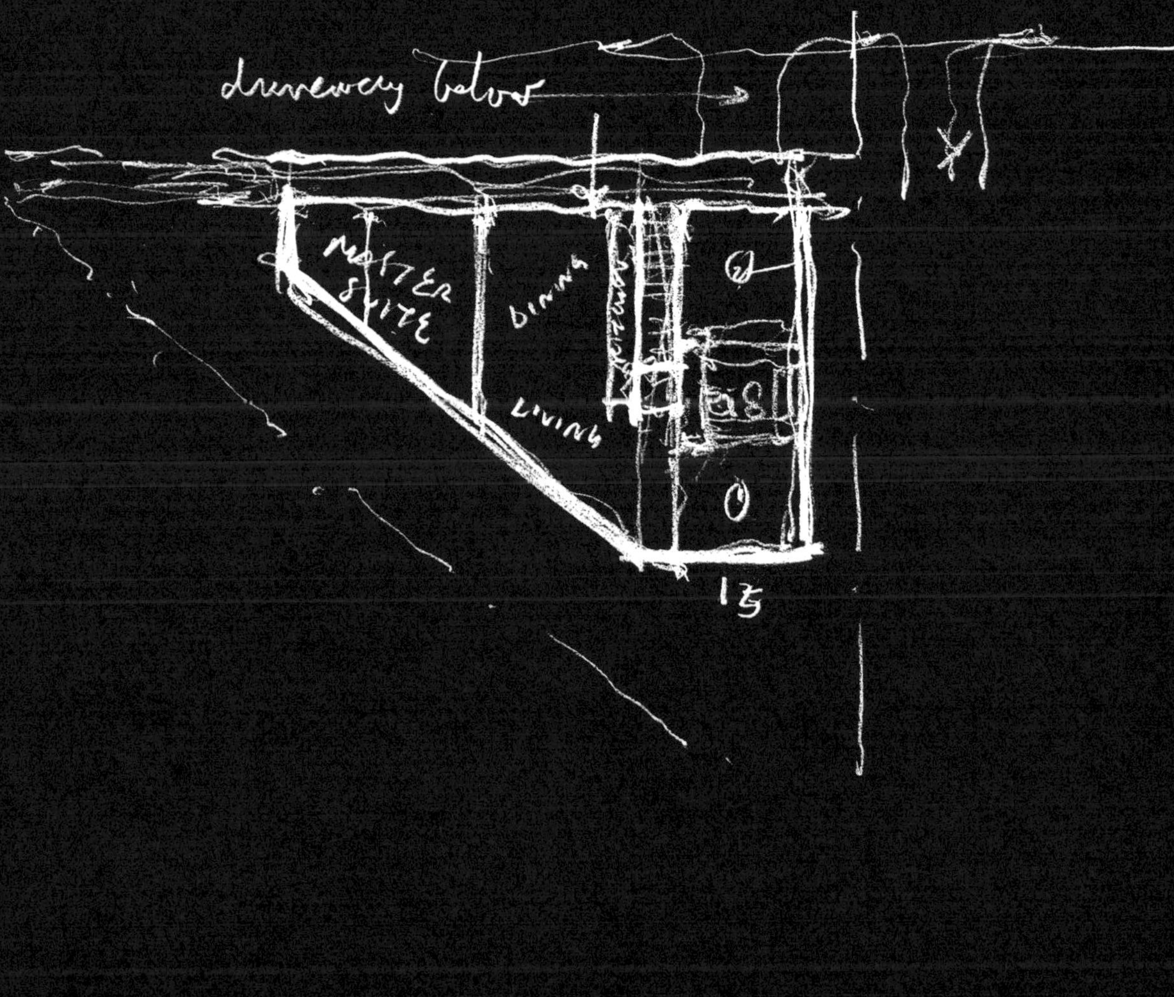
driveway below
MASTER SUITE
DINING
LIVING

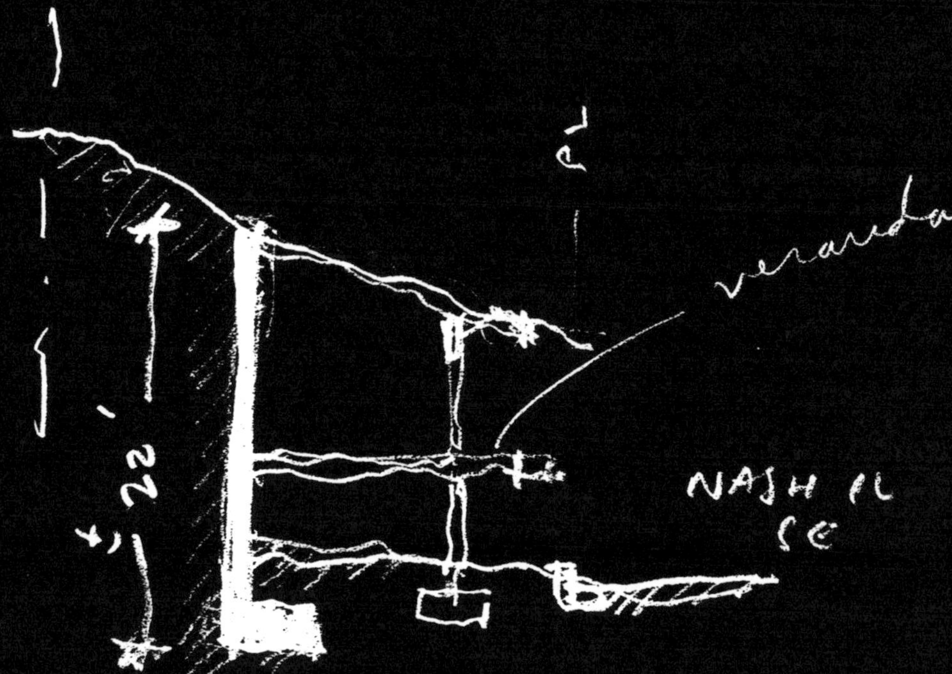
veranda
22'

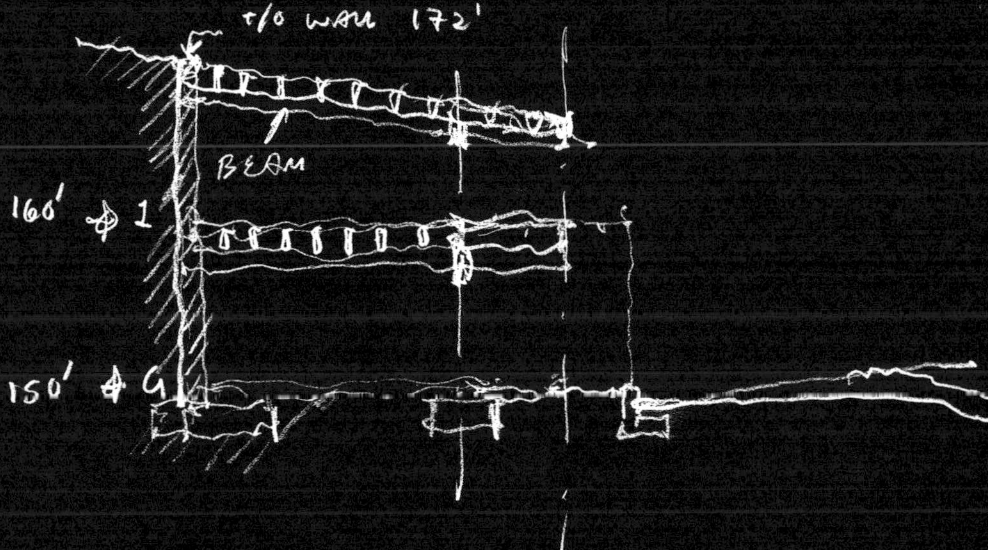
T/O WALL 172'
BEAM
160' ⌀ 1
150' ⌀ G

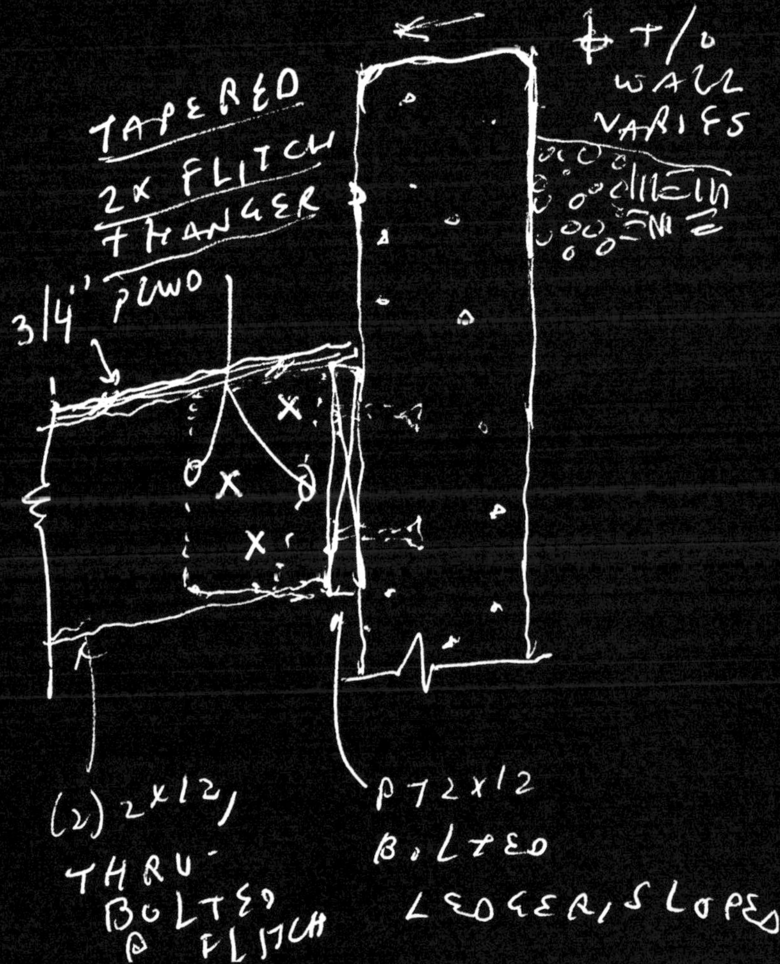
TAPERED
2x FLITCH
+ HANGER
3/4" PLWD
T/O
WALL
VARIES
(2) 2x12,
THRU-
BOLTED
@ FLITCH
PT 2x12
BOLTED
LEDGER, SLOPED

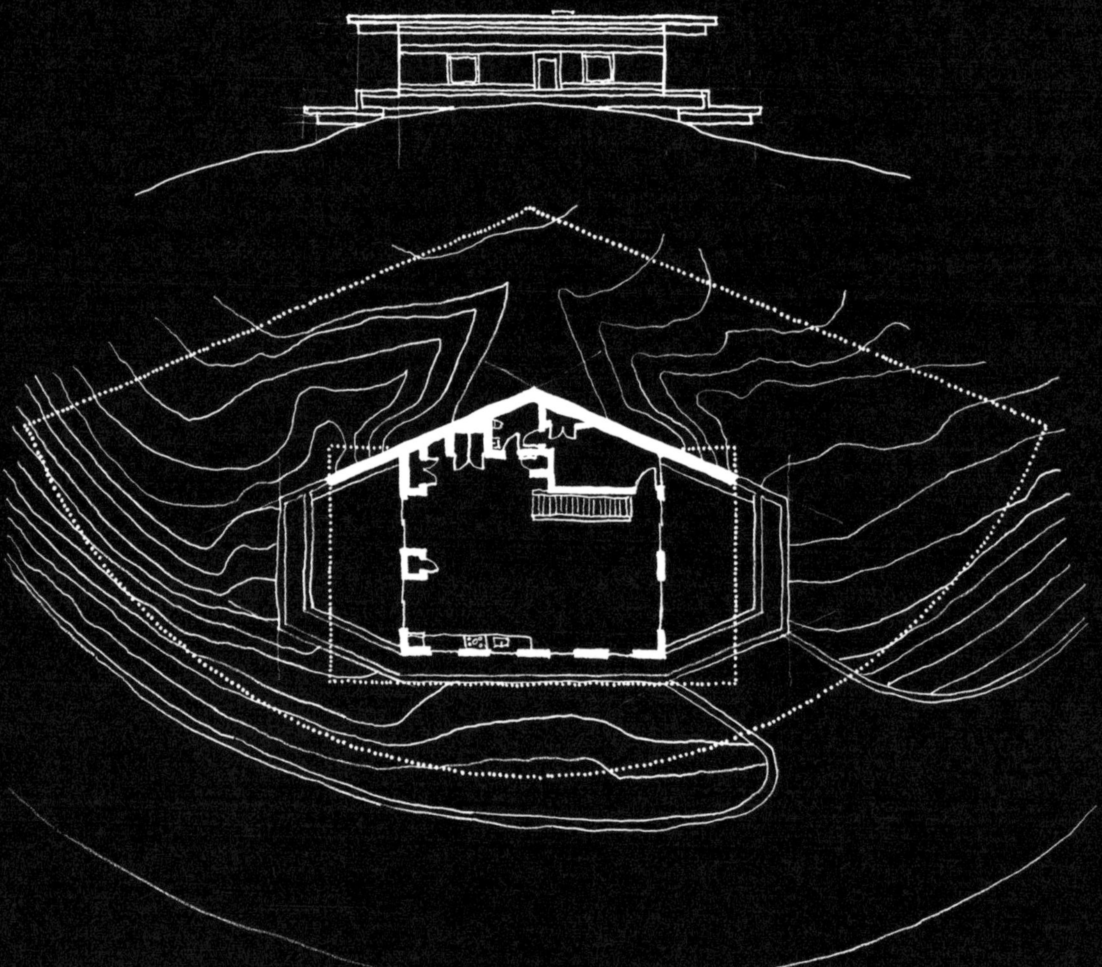

TEMPLE HOUSE

Westover, Washington, DC

On a proud bluff overlooking the city, combine:

1 heavily reinforced retaining wall
1 precut BamCore kit
Equal parts BamCore kit to wool insulation
A few truckloads of 3x12 glulam joists
A few large DLT floor slabs
Some cork flooring
Equal parts cork and charred cypress cladding
Black locust planter boxes and decking
Some grasses, herbs, sedum, and soil trays
Solar array
Some skylights
Some exterior glass doors
Some awning windows
Brass fixtures, handles, and pulls

---

1. Stabilize the slope; excavate and construct the retaining wall. Use the soil at another project.

2. Assemble, stuff, and dress BamCore panels.

3. Connect the floors and roofs. Top with green roofs, planter boxes, black locust decking, and solar array.

4. Slot in windows, doors, skylights, stairs.

5. Stack alternating layers of cork and charred cypress cladding.

6. Orient interiors toward preferred views.

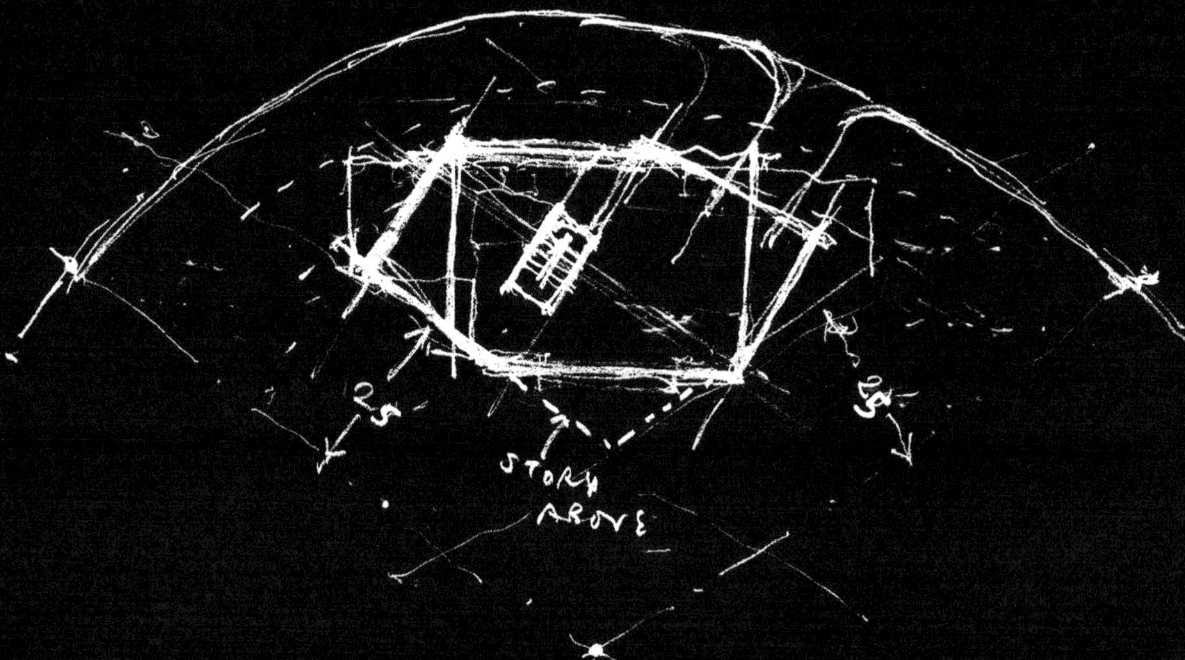

25
25
STORY
ABOVE

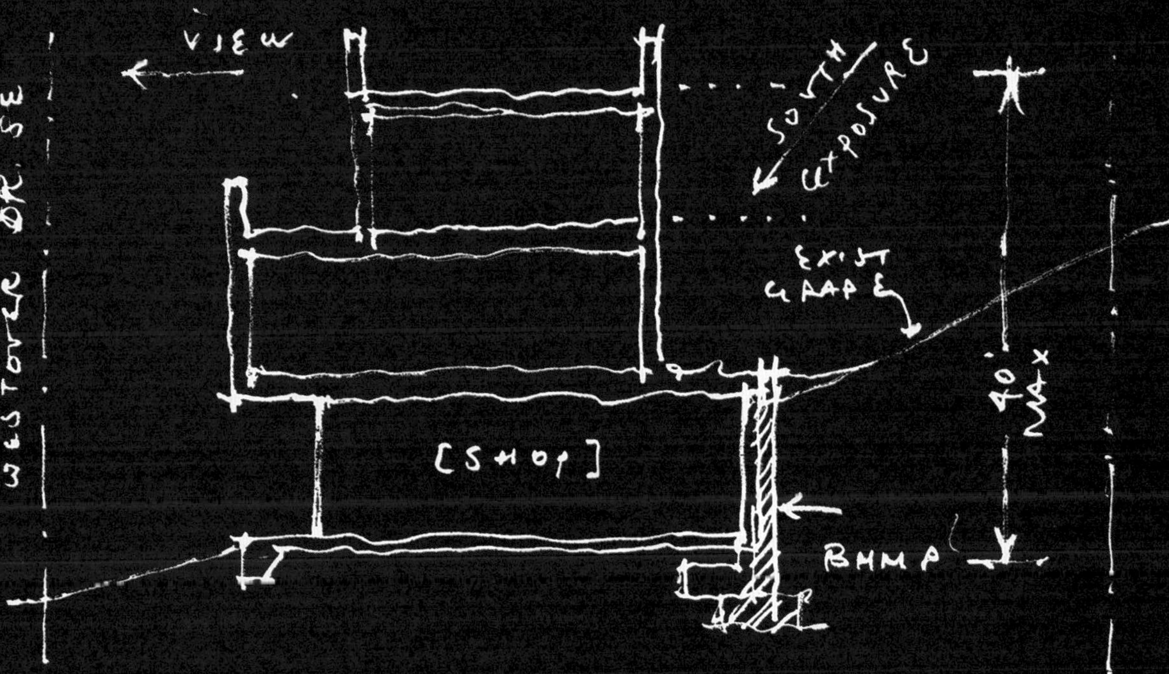
VIEW
SOUTH EXPOSURE
WESTOVER DR. SE
EXIST GRADE
[SHOP]
40' MAX

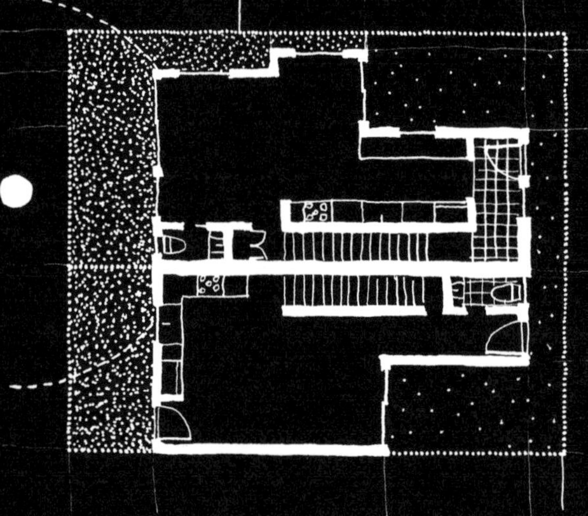

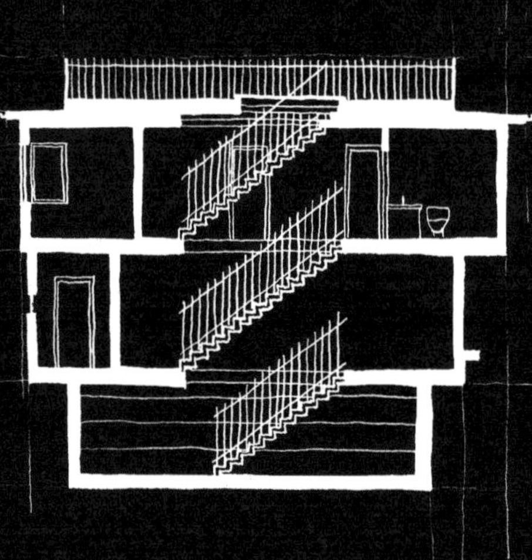

SPLIT HOUSE

Capitol Hill, Washington, DC

On a pair of inconspicuous, seemingly too-small parcels
at the back of an old alley, combine:

2 basements built with Omni Block masonry units
1 precut BamCore kit
Equal parts BamCore kit to wool insulation
A few truckbeds of 2x10 floor joists
Bundles of cedar beams and sticks
Bundles of black locust beams and sticks
1 tub of spray cork
Some cork siding
Some cork flooring
Some black locust roof decking
Some exterior glass doors
Some awning windows
Brass fixtures, handles, and pulls
A few rolls of bronze insect screening

---

1. Scoop out soil and construct the basements and foundations. Use the soil at another project.

2. Frame the walls, floors, and roofs; top with a thin, eaved roof.

3. Sprinkle with windows, doors, stairs.

4. Surround the exterior walls in cork; wrap balconies in bronze screen.

5. Insert stair and cap with roof guardrails.

6. Add kitchens and bath components. Coat interior in spray cork.

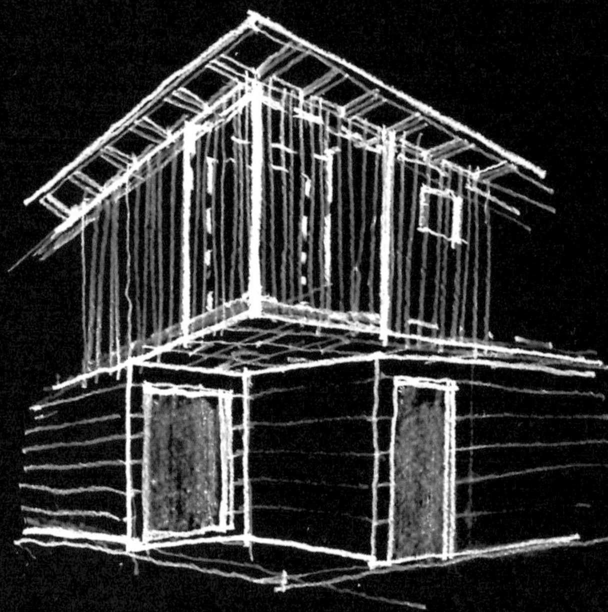

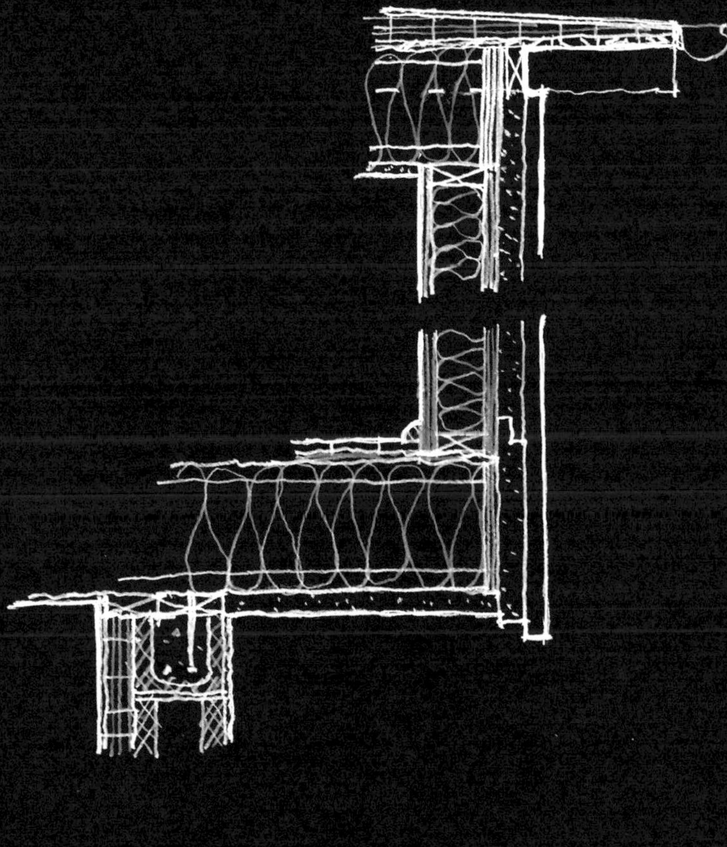

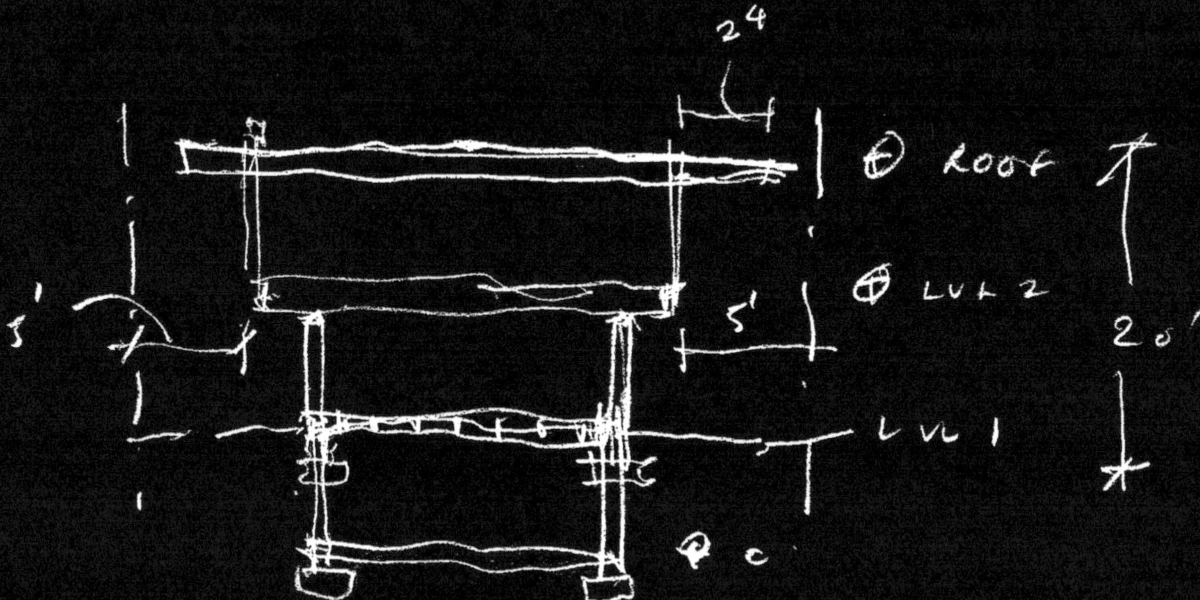
24"
ROOF
LVL 2
5'
5'
20'
LVL 1

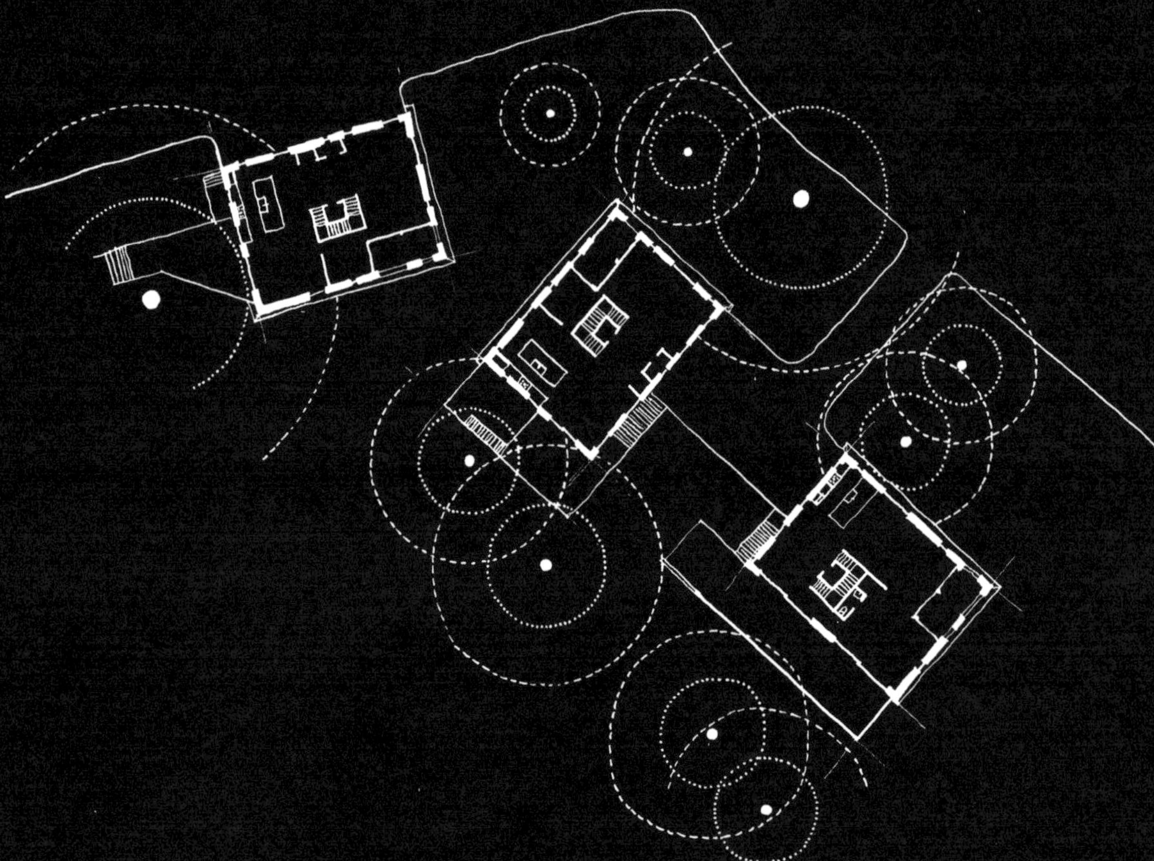

BROAD HOUSES

Broad Branch, Washington, DC

At the bottom of a ravine along a surprisingly busy street, combine:

3 precut BamCore kits
Equal parts BamCore kit to cellulose insulation
Cedar beams and sticks
Oak sticks, rough sawn
A dozen bundles of willow
1 part cork siding : 1 part charred cedar boards : 1 part bark siding
A few rolls of copper insect screening and copper flashing
Some oak flooring, quarter sawn
Some skylights, exterior glass doors, and awning windows
Some black locust decking
A baker's dozen truckloads of local rocks roughly 1 cu ft in size

---

1. Pour three foundations and allow to set. On top of them, make ground floors out of Omni Block masonry units. Stack local rocks against the Omni Block.

2. Lift, wrap, and stuff the BamCore panels. Sprinkle copper flashing and screening throughout.

3. Top with roof, black locust decking, and planter boxes.

4. Dress each BamCore frame in either cork, bark, or cedar.

5. Infuse with windows, doors, skylights, stairs.

6. Decorate interior.

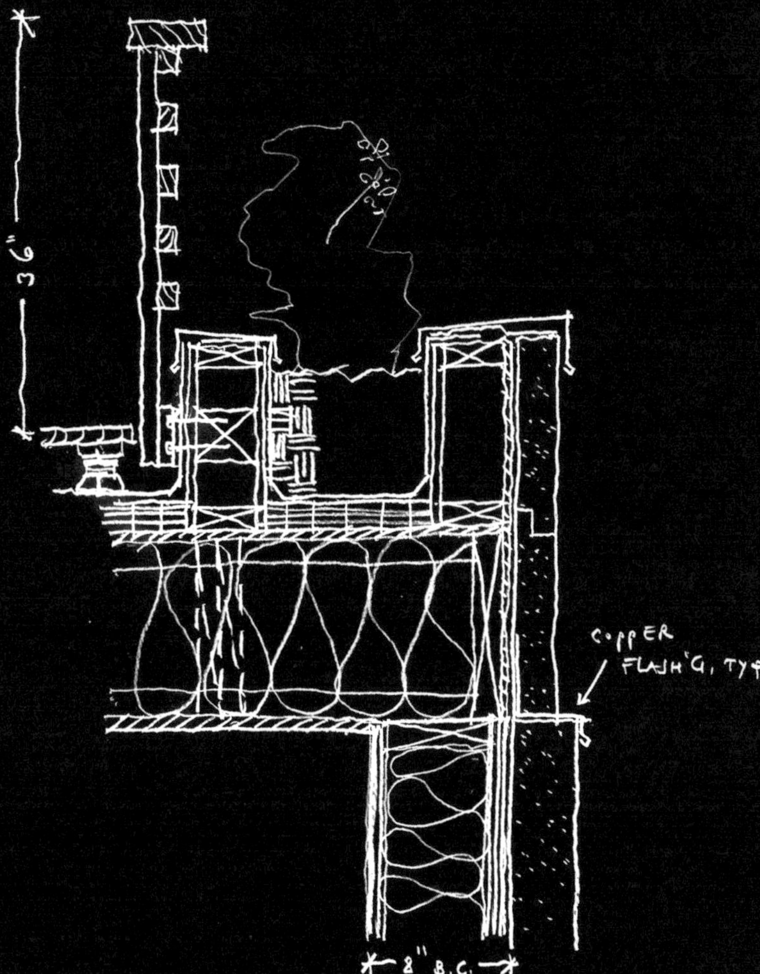
3'6"
COPPER
FLASH'G, TYP
8" B.C.

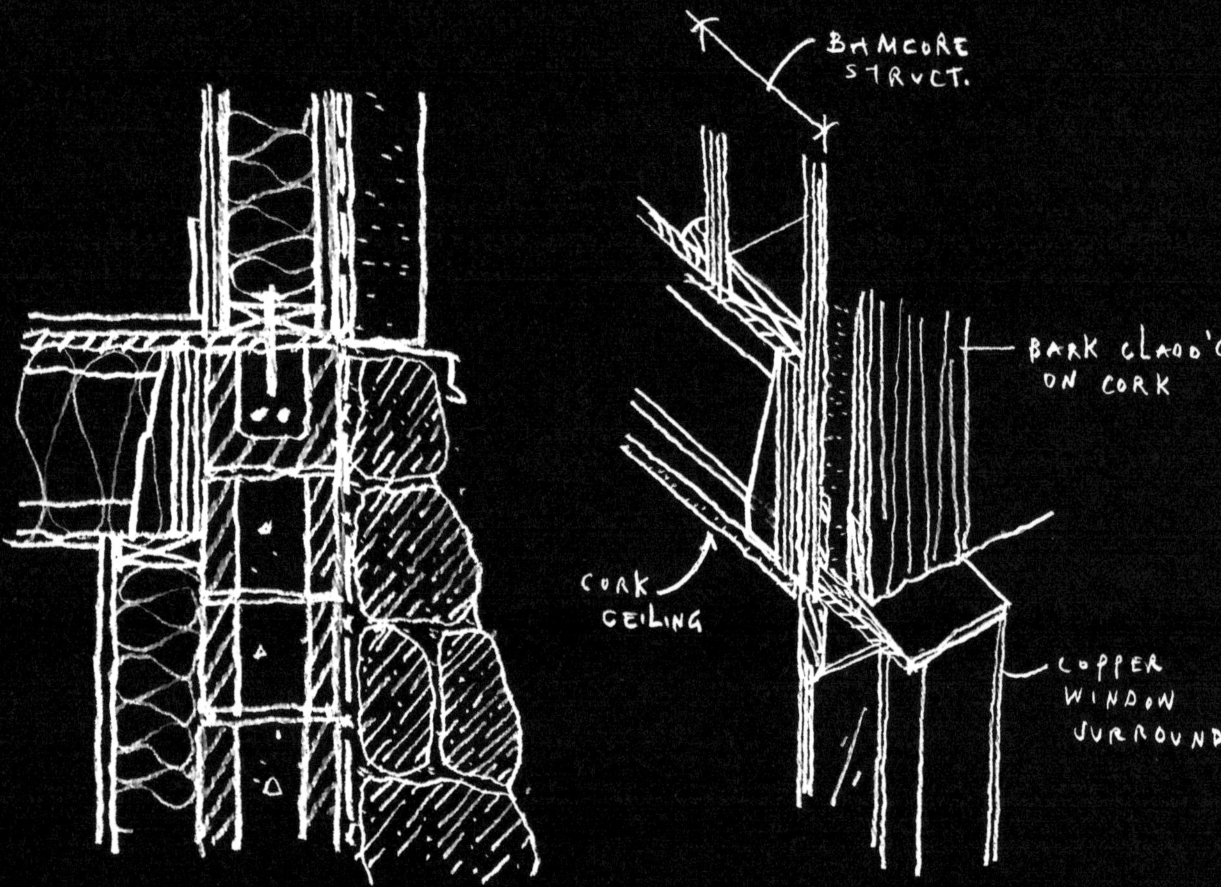
BAMCORE STRUCT.
BARK CLADD'G ON CORK
CORK CEILING
COPPER WINDOW SURROUND

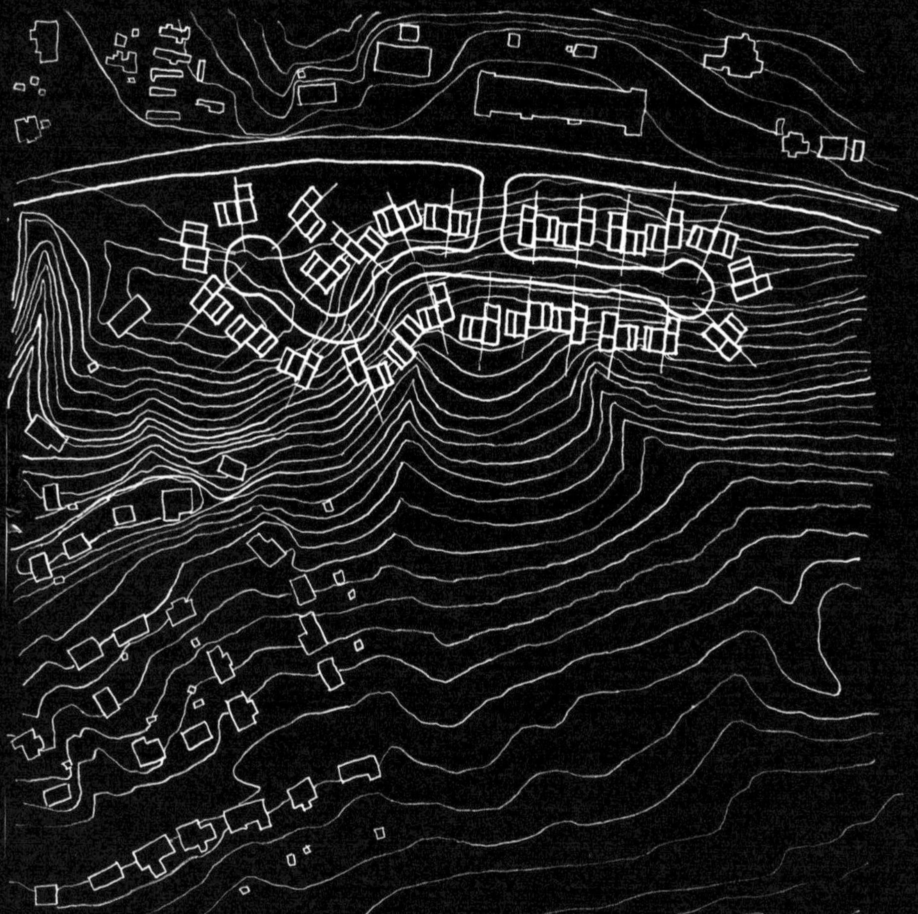

SPARROWS

Shenandoah River, VA

On the crest of a river's edge with an expansive view, combine:

Hundreds of helical piles
25 precut BamCore kits
Equal parts BamCore kit to wool insulation
Dozens of big glulam joists
Some oak flooring
Some interior-finish spray cork
Some cedar cladding and roof shingles
Some exterior glass doors
Some awning windows
Brass fixtures, handles, and pulls
25 copper gutters and rain chains

---

1. Mash helical piles into the sloped terrain to create a platform for each house with minimal land disturbance.

2. Assemble and stuff BamCore panels and frame the floors and roofs. Cap with overhanging roof eaves and dress with cedar shingles.

3. Gradually add windows, doors, skylights, stairs.

4. Top with copper gutters and rain chains.

5. Gently fold in kitchens and baths.
   Smother hempboard partitions and ceilings with spray cork.

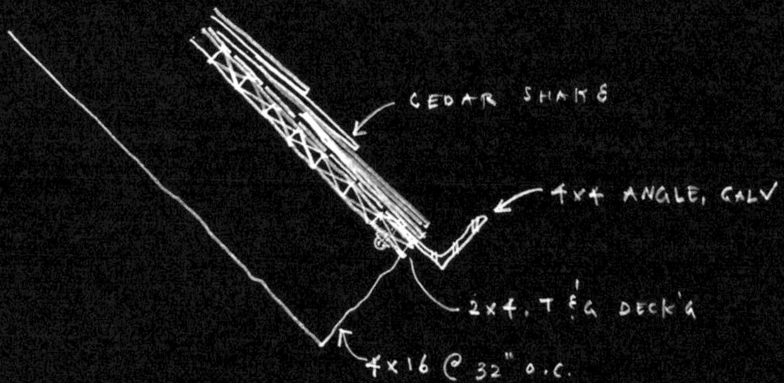
CEDAR SHAKE
4x4 ANGLE, GALV
2x4, T&G DECK'G
4x16 @ 32" O.C.

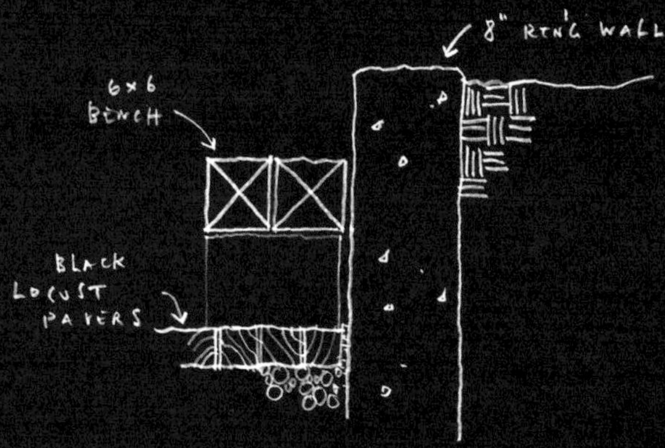
8" RTN'G WALL
6x6
BENCH
BLACK
LOCUST
PAVERS

ON THE HOUSE

"The overarching role of the Office of the Parliamentarian is to strive for consistency in parliamentary analysis by attempting to apply pertinent precedent to each procedural question... This fidelity to precedent promotes analytic consistency and procedural predictability and thereby fosters legitimacy in parliamentary practice."

- The House Practice:
A Guide to the Rules, Precedents and Procedures of the House

The House Practice is the rulebook that organizes the functions of the US Congress and the Senate—the lineaments that structure America's political debates and dialogues. Organized around a collection of precedents, this archive of instances facilitates the continual design of a nation, (theoretically) setting the table for convivial dialogue.

BLDUS houses are similarly anchored in a quintessentially American lineage of (architectural) precedents that connect tradition with progress organically: a classic architecture rooted in common practice in a shared country.

By contending with conventions of domesticity, these houses strive for timeless qualities of harmonious habitation. Prioritizing climatic elements like wind, sun, and rain, and built from minimally processed materials, they reorient their inhabitants to connect with the nature found in their urban environments. Like *The House Practice*, *Home on Earth* provides a blueprint for continuity with the past through precedent.

Long House
Swampy Hollow
Wide House
Broad Houses
Thick House
Split House
Poplar Grove
Temple House
Ramble House
Grass House
Poplar Cloud
Sparrows

Grass House

Stick House

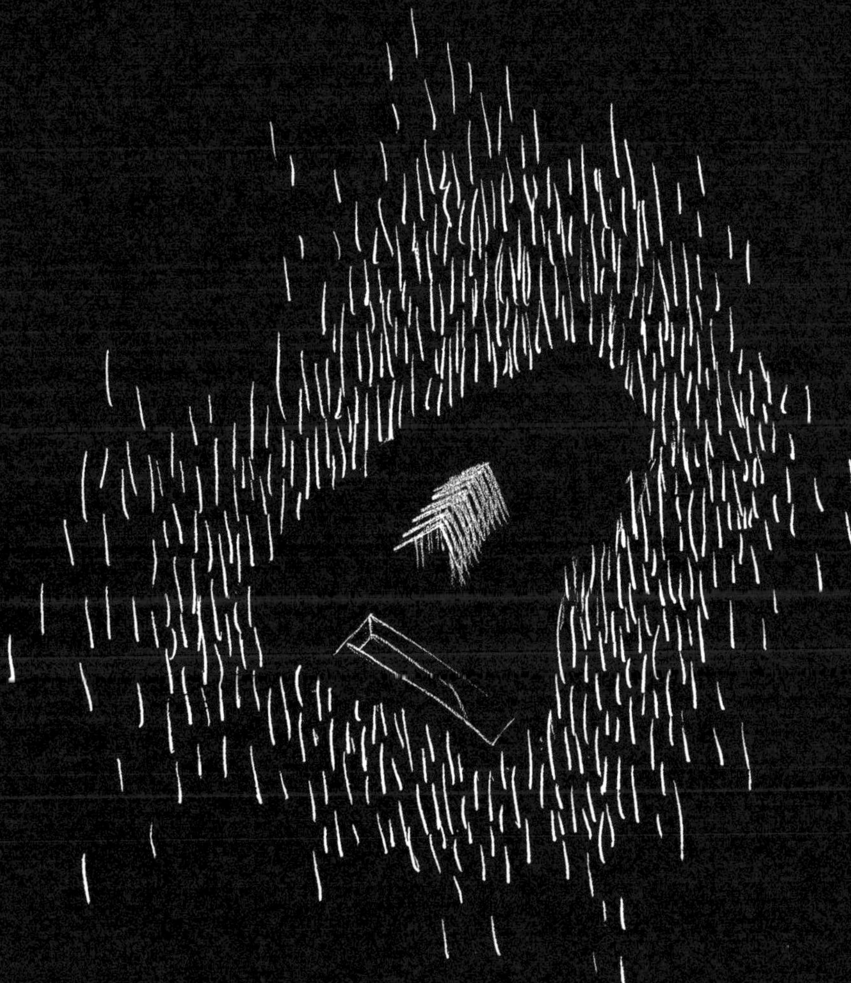

Poplar Cloud

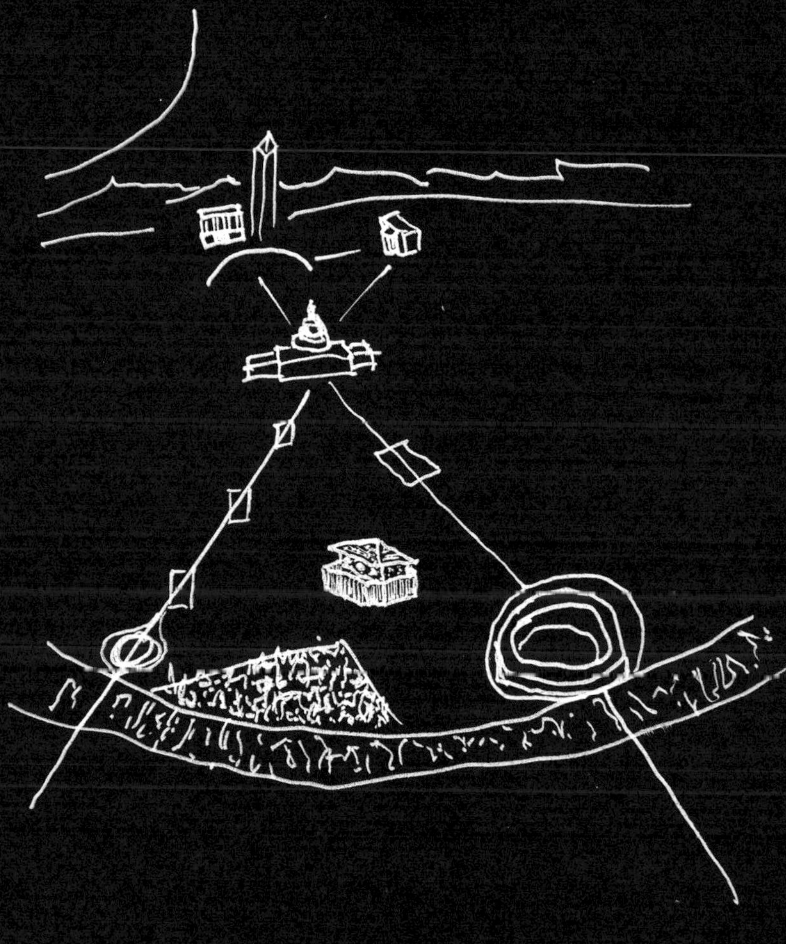

Wide House

Brown House

Long House

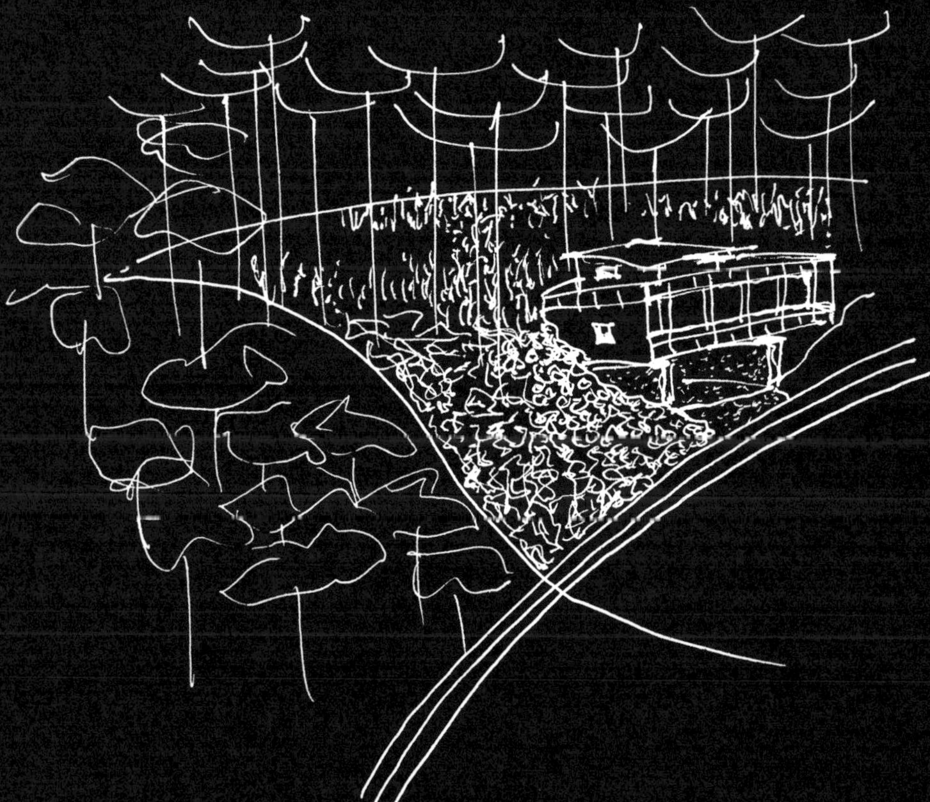

Temple House

Split House

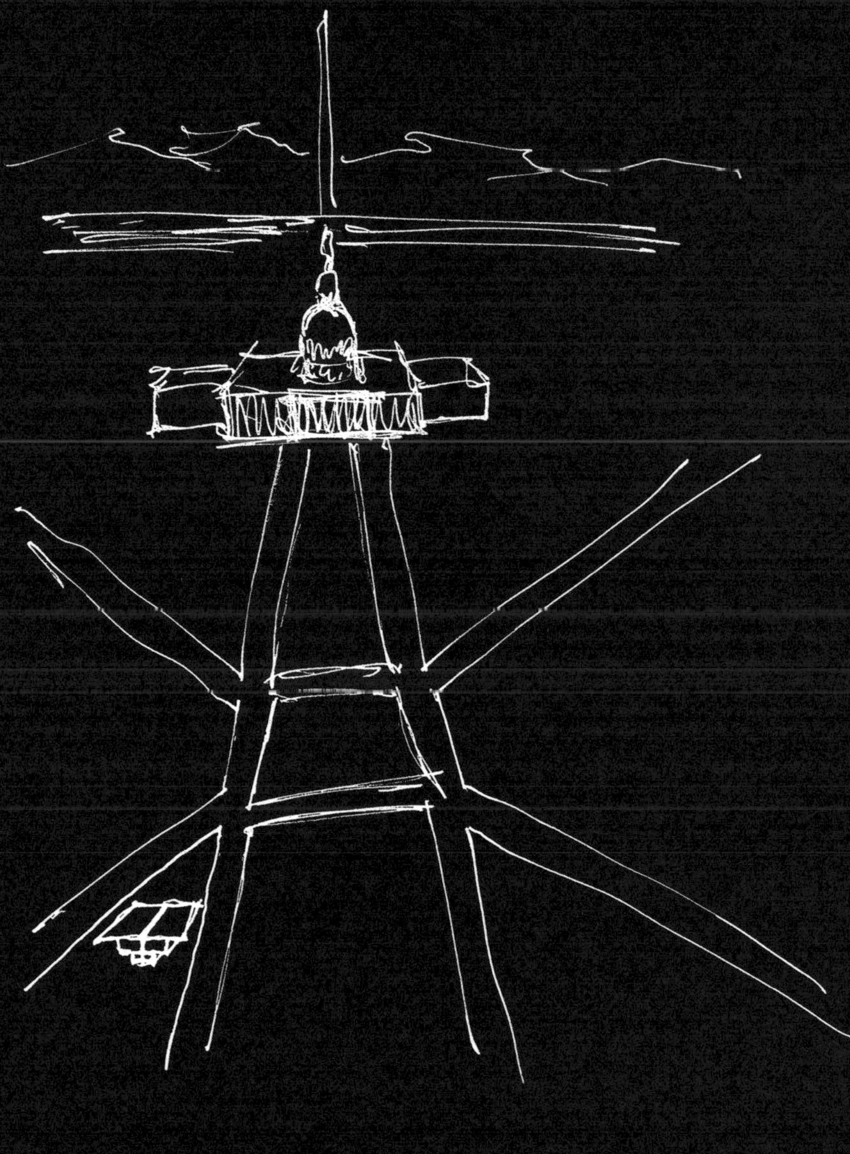

Broad Houses

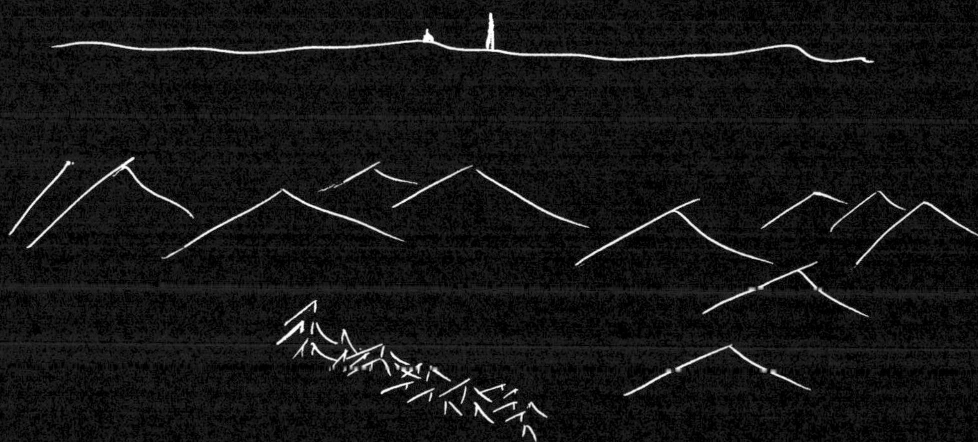

BIOGRAPHIES

BLDUS

BLDUS is an architecture and development office founded by Jack Becker and Andrew Linn in 2013. Adam Ainslie has been a contributor since 2020. Based in Washington, DC, BLDUS creates an architecture of accommodation that pays tribute to its context and gains integrity as it ages.

BLDUS seeks opportunities in economies of scale, scope, density, means, and materials, often integrating traditional construction methods with new technologies and organic materials ideally suited to their region.

BLDUS has taught at Virginia Tech, the University of Maryland, and the Catholic University of America and has been honored with a 2019 Architect's Newspaper's Young Architect Award, a 2021 AIA Young Architect Award, a 2023 Architectural Record Design Vanguard Award, and AIA Chapter Design Awards.

TY COLE

Ty Cole is an award-winning photographer who is driven by a passion for design and technology, and a curiosity about how humans connect with each other and their environments, built or natural.
This passion has led to a career collaborating with renowned design firms, publications, and corporate brands. His work is a hybrid of technical acuity and spontaneity, creating images that are bold yet nuanced.

ACKNOWLEDGMENTS

THANK YOU

Jim Bassett
Nancy Becker
Richard Becker
Erlend Blakstad Haffner
Suzanne Cody
Michael Corcoran
Carl Elefante
Bernardo Fort Brescia
Sassan Gharai
Rem Koolhaas
Paul Lewis
Lu Liu
Ruben Lopez
Håkon Matre Aasarød
Margaret McCurry
Ronnie McGhee
Michael Meredith
Susan Piedmont-Palladino
Steve Schwat
Charlie Sleichter
Laurinda Spear

Danielle Barberini
Julian Barberini
Alexsis Blakely
Adolfo Briceño
Brad Collins
Marie Collins
Monica Dalvi
Devonte Dinkins
Martin Ditto
Ryan Eshelman
Koura Gibson
Nya Gill
Ivan Iricanin
Nick Keenan
K Leszczak
Cherie McCord
Diarra McKinney
Bob Pincus
Susan Pincus
Andrew Prins
Ryan Segars

Stan Allen
Paul Anderson
Melinda Becker
Lily Chi
Keller Easterling
Peter Eisenman
Paul Emmons
el-Hadi Jaizery
Christoph Kumpusch
Mark Morris
Paul Masi
Forrest Meegers
Alicia Moreira
Monica Ponce de León
Kathie Prigmore
Bill Rankin
David Salmela
Hashim Sarkis
Suman Seth
Bob Stern
Jonathan Tate

ORO EDITIONS

Publishers of Architecture, Art, and Design
Gordon Goff: Publisher

www.oroeditions.com
info@oroeditions.com

Published by ORO Editions

ISBN: 978-1-961856-51-6

BLDUS

TY COLE

Graphic Design: BLDUS
Graphic Identity: Studio Lin
Photographs (All Except Stick House): Ty Cole
Photographs (Stick House): Michael Vahrenwald
ORO Managing Editor: Kirby Anderson

10 9 8 7 6 5 4 3 2 1 First Edition

Library of Congress data available upon request. World Rights: Available

Color Separations and Printing: ORO Editions, Inc. Printed in China.

International Distribution: www.oroeditions.com/distribution

ORO Editions makes a continuous effort to minimize the overall carbon footprint of its publications. As part of this goal, ORO Editions, in association with Global ReLeaf, arranges to plant trees to replace those used in the manufacturing of the paper produced for its books. Global ReLeaf is an international campaign run by American Forests, one of the world's oldest nonprofit conservation organizations. Global ReLeaf is American Forests' education and action program that helps individuals, organizations, agencies, and corporations improve the local and global environment by planting and caring for trees.

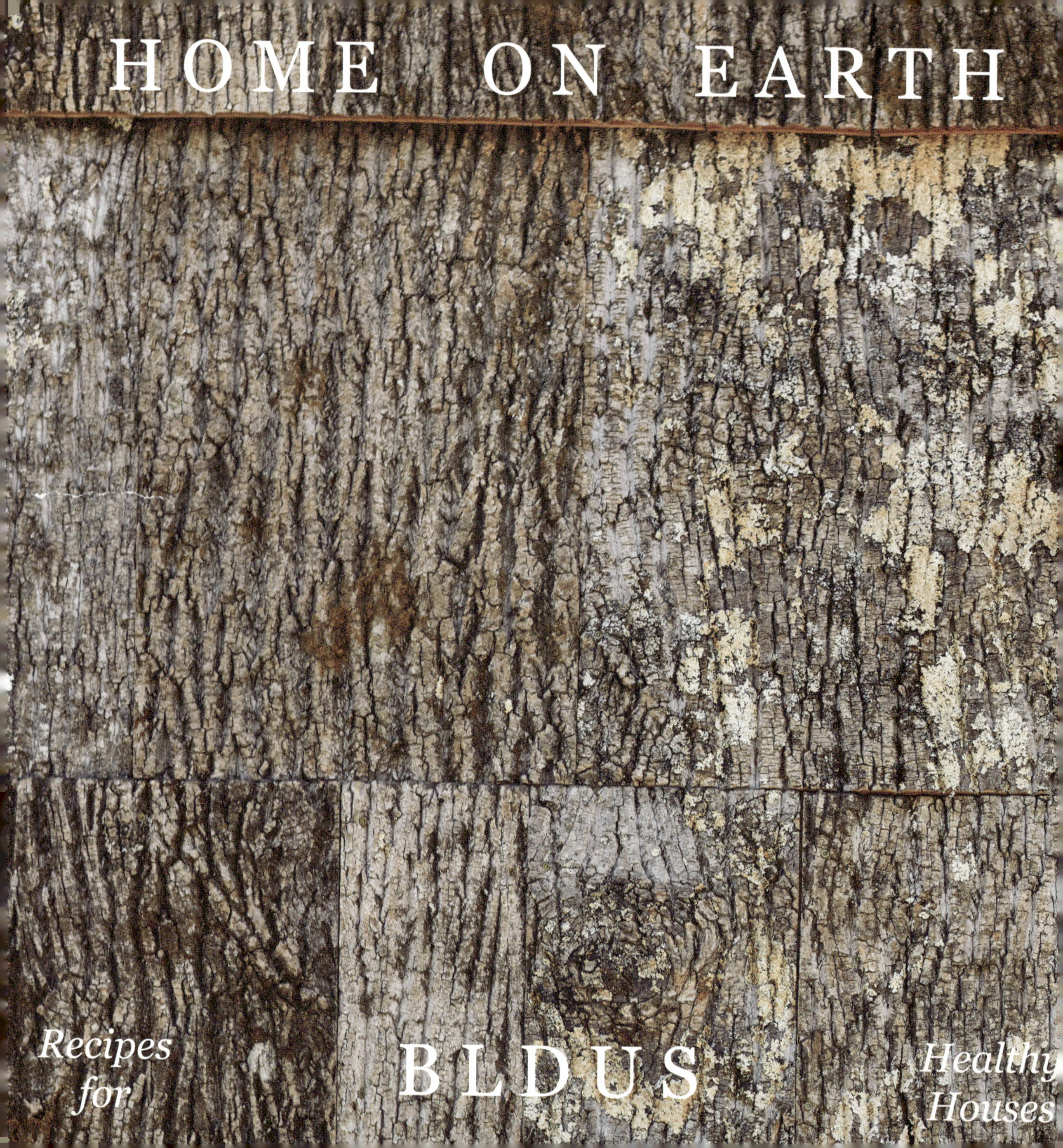
HOME ON EARTH
Recipes for
BLDUS
Healthy Houses